HOSTEEN KLAH

Navaho Medicine Man and Sand Painter

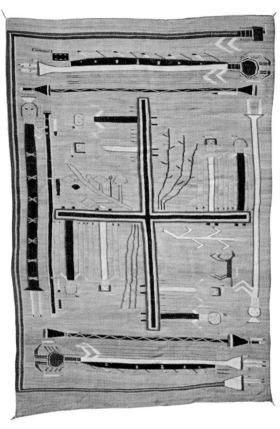

THE WHIRLING LOG DESIGN
First Sand Painting Tapestry
Woven by Hosteen Klah

HOSTEEN KLAH

Navaho Medicine Man and Sand Painter

By Franc Johnson Newcomb

UNIVERSITY OF OKLAHOMA PRESS : NORMAN

By Franc Johnson Newcomb

Sandpaintings of the Navajo Shooting Chant (with
    Gladys A. Reichard) (New York, 1937)
Navajo Omens and Taboos (Santa Fe, 1940)
A Study of Navajo Symbolism (with Stanley Fishler and
    Mary C. Wheelwright) (Cambridge, 1956)
Hosteen Klah: Navaho Medicine Man and Sand Painter
    (Norman, 1964)
Navaho Neighbors (Norman, 1966)

Library of Congress Catalog Card Number: 64–20759

Copyright 1964 by the University of Oklahoma Press, Publishing Division
of the University. Manufactured in the U.S.A. First edition, October, 1964;
second printing, January, 1971.

DEDICATED
To The Memory of ARTHUR JOHN NEWCOMB

Foreword

LUCY G. BLOOMFIELD

WHEN MY LONG-TIME FRIEND, Franc J. Newcomb, wrote to say she was thinking of writing an account of our yesterdays among our Indian friends on the Navaho Reservation and would like to have me write the Foreword, I was pleased, as I could immediately think of many things to be said. I appreciate the privilege of writing briefly about my friend, Franc, and about our mutual friend, the noted medicine man, Hosteen Klah; and as I write, more and more memories come to mind of bygone days on the Reservation and of the Navaho friends who lived all around us.

My husband, George R. Bloomfield, and I, together with our eight children, owned a trading post at Toadlena, which we had purchased in 1911. In 1914 a family by the name of Newcomb bought the trading post at Pesh-do-clish, which was later named "Newcomb" when a U.S. post office was established there.

It was with joy we met and became acquainted with this family, and soon acquaintance ripened into a firm friendship. The Newcombs were our neighbors in a vast, lonesome land. The thirteen miles between us did not deter us from being neighborly, and many were the good times, family parties, and picnics we enjoyed together. Our eight children, the Newcomb two, and our other neighbors, Pearl and Ed Davies, who lived halfway between us at Two Grey Hills with their three children, met for these affairs. Then there were the missionary's five children, and when they joined us, it was quite a gathering; and none of the children felt iso-

lated from children of their own race. Sometimes we pic-
nicked on the mountain back of our post, sometimes at the
foot of Two Grey Hills where the youngsters climbed the
steep mesa sides, and in cooler weather we built our picnic
fires out on the flats. The missionaries were the Reverend
and Mrs. Brink, and later the Reverend and Mrs. Kobes.

Schooling for our children was a big problem on the
Reservation. We were lucky in that the missionary had several children, who, added to our school-age ones, enabled
us to demand a country school, which was granted after
many excuses and delays. The Newcomb children were
especially lucky, for their mother had been a schoolteacher
four years in her home town, two years at the Indian school
at Keshena, Wisconsin, and then at the Navaho Government
School at Fort Defiance. Since Mrs. Newcomb had been a
primary teacher, she was qualified to give her children their
first years of schooling.

The Newcombs were the kind of neighbors who, when
they moved to Farmington to put their older girl into high
school, took my daughter Ruthie, who was in the same grade
as Lynette, and treated her as one of their own. Later they
moved to Albuquerque and again took Ruthie with them—
"friends in need."

I am sure one reason I loved Franc Newcomb was that
she regarded the Navaho people the same way I did. To us
they were not just "wild" or "tame" Indians. They were just
what their Navaho name says, "The Dinnae," meaning "The
People." In their own estimation, they were every bit as important as white people, and so they carried themselves with
pride and dignity. Of course, we found both good and bad
among them, but the bad were a small percentage.

The Newcombs had their "grand old man," Hosteen Klah—"Azaethlin" (medicine man), as the Navahos called him—who lived near their trading post. We had our "grand old man," Natana, "Chief," as his name implies, who lived near our trading post. These two prominent Navaho men definitely exploded the old myth that " a dead Indian is the only good Indian." These two not only lived good lives, but did their utmost to help their people live better lives. And so I am pleased that Klah's biography has now been written to follow the book I have written about Chief Natana.

I have attended many "sings," as the white people call almost all Navaho ceremonies, and have seen the perfect accord with which Klah and Natana worked together. At a given signal, which I always failed to catch, Klah and his helpers would stop their chants and ritual, and Natana would step forth into the firelight. You could hear a pin drop, if there had been a floor instead of sand to drop it on. Then Natana would orate for about an hour or so to the crowd assembled for the sing, which was sometimes only a few hundred and sometimes more than a thousand, depending on the importance of the ceremony.

Natana would tell the people to pay attention to the medicine man and to have faith in him because he had much power with the Great Spirit and was praying for the recovery of the one for whom the ceremony was being held. He would then instruct his people how to live to gain the blessing they desired and close his harangue with this admonition: "Do not drink that bad firewater the white man tries to sell you! It will make you crazy in the head, bad in your actions, and your money will be gone for worse than nothing." Both he and Klah practiced what they preached and were both "good" Indians and "live" Indians.

It always takes a few years for the Navahos to come to trust and like the white people who come among them, but when they decide to like a person, they grant him many favors denied to others who are not so fortunate. This great privilege was granted to both Mr. and Mrs. Newcomb and to us. The Navahos invited us to attend their ceremonies, and thus we profited in that we came to know the people themselves and to have some knowledge of their inner lives and their great faith as expressed through their sand paintings and religious rites.

Franc Newcomb had a great talent for mentally recording the things she saw and heard. She could take a "mind picture" of a sand painting and later transfer it to paper with all its color and detail correct; and so today the wonderful sand paintings made by Hosteen Klah on the smooth floor of the ceremonial hogan are preserved for Navaho posterity which would otherwise have been lost at his passing. This was an unusual gift granted to Mrs. Newcomb, and she did not hide it under a bushel or bury it in the earth, but used it to collect more than 450 sand-painting sketches. She also used the knowledge gained to write articles and books on Navaho lore. She has written *Navajo Omens and Taboos, Sandpaintings of the Navajo Shooting Chant, A Study of Navajo Symbolism,* and "Origin Legend of the Navajo Eagle Chant."

After I had attended a particularly impressive Navaho ceremony, I was led to exclaim, "Who are we to say that our conventional way of praying is the only way a prayer can reach the Throne on High!" I have witnessed healing right before my eyes. One case was that of a young Navaho wife who had been educated in the government school, then came home and was married. When she became ill, she first went to white doctors, three of whom said she could not be cured and had only a short time to live. In desperation she and her parents and friends called a medicine man and had a healing ceremony held for her. She recovered, had two children, and died eight years later of a very different malady. The faith of these Navahos and the power of their medicine men is not often understood by white people.

The other neighboring family which I mentioned earlier, Mr. and Mrs. Ed Davies, owned and operated a trading post midway between ours at Toadlena and the Newcomb Post at Pesh-do-clish. All three of us worked with the Navaho weavers to help them improve their rugs, which in time came to be called the "Two Grey Hills Rugs" and still are known far and wide for their fine weave and the beauty of their design. These brought the highest prices of any rugs woven on the Reservation, with the exception of the sand-painting tapestries woven by Klah and his immediate family. It was also the traders who encouraged the Navahos to improve their livestock so that their wool clip would be of better quality and bring them more money, and it was the traders who found a market for their silverwork.

The annual Navaho Fair, started by Superintendent W. T. Shelton at the Shiprock Agency, was a great day for traders and Indians. There was an exhibit building in which every trader had a booth to display the products and arts of his Navaho customers. Prizes were given for the best displays and for top articles displayed, and no hard feelings were ever entertained against those who received the prizes. It was a great incentive for the Navahos to improve the quality of their product. During the daytime the Indians enjoyed a rodeo and horse racing; at night there was always an authentic Yeibichai all could attend. One of the unusual features of the Shiprock Fair was "Watermelon Day." The Indian School Farm raised quantities of watermelons, and the day before the fair, Superintendent Shelton would have many wagonloads of the ripest piled in the center of the athletic field. Just at noon of the second day word would be sent around that the feast was about to begin. Hundreds of Indians would gather around the mountain of melons and select the ones they wanted. They were privileged to take any number, but they must eat them there. What a sight that was! I have often wondered how many small children ended up with stomach-aches.

Now that our paths of life have led us away from the Reservation, Mrs. Newcomb to Albuquerque and me to Farmington, we find that we suffer at times from nostalgia for "The People," who were our friends and neighbors as well as our customers. However, we can both sleep well at night because our consciences do not bother us. We did not cheat them at trading, and we did try to help them in many ways. We have our reward when we meet the ones we knew years ago and they call us "Tse-kis," My Friend.

Both Klah and Natana have been gone for many years but they are not forgotten, either by their own people or by the many other persons whose lives were enriched by their friendship.

Introduction

For some years it has been my ambition to write at least a portion of the biography of Hosteen Klah, the noted medicine man, wealthy stockman, and unsurpassed weaver who played such an important role in our lives while we were living on the Navaho Reservation. During the quarter of a century my husband, myself, and our two children owned and operated the Pesh-do-clish trading post, Klah with his clan family were our neighbors, our helpers, and our best friends. It was through his influence that I was able to attend Navaho religious ceremonies, and it was with his permission that I started making sketches of his sacred sand paintings. Although we did not realize it at the time we started our trading post, the land on which our buildings were located was part of the domain over which his great-grandfather, Chief Narbona, had ruled and might be considered part of Klah's inheritance.

Klah told us that his ancestors had come from the north to these blue mountains seven generations before his birth to find them uninhabited, well watered, and abounding in game animals. So here they had built their hogans and established rights to water, fields, and hunting areas. It was from this location their women had acquired the clan name of Tzith-ah-ni, meaning "Brow of the Mountain," as it was always the women who chose the places to live and it was through the women that clan names and property rights descended generation after generation. The seven generations Klah mentioned cannot be easily translated into years, as his Navaho word could also be translated as meaning seven lifetimes, which would be a much longer period.

During our early years at the post, Klah, his mother, and his sister and her four daughters were living two or three miles east of us in a cluster of hogans built at the edge of their cornfields. They were one of the wealthiest Navaho families living in our valley, owning more than two thousand sheep and a number of cattle and horses. As they were frequent customers at our store, we soon became friends and visited back and forth, Klah always inviting us to any special occasions. It was then I became interested in learning more of the history of this group of Navahos among whom we were living, especially of its older members. Nearly all of these "Old Ones" had lived through the period of soldier oppression, taken the long walk to the Bosque Redondo, and returned to a ravaged land.

How they managed to be such an industrious, good-natured people and still friendly to the whites was amazing to me after hearing the personal stories of hardship, persecution, slavery, semistarvation, and heroic self-denial they were almost afraid to tell. I could hardly believe some of the events related, but I found them corroborated in war records, old government bulletins, and histories of the Navaho people. These gave me the names of the places and the people connected with these events and the dates they took place. I decided it would be interesting to record the personal stories of eight of our oldest Navaho neighbors. The central theme would be their recollections of the trip to the Bosque Redondo, the lives they led while there, and then their return to their homeland.

Klah's mother, nearing eighty years of age but still remarkably active and as mentally alert as any of her grand-children, was the first person I approached on the subject. It was not difficult to gain her consent, for her great-grand-daughter, Lucy Hapaha, was living with us that summer as housemaid and could serve as interpreter, so the old lady did not feel that she was telling her story to strangers. The recording occupied several afternoons, and I have used it as a chapter in this book, quoting her story exactly as it was given to me by Lucy, with only a few explanations regarding names and places added. She even allowed me to take her picture when the story was finished, a privilege few of the older Navahos would grant.

After we had completed this story, we interviewed Bit-see Lakai (Gray Hair), who was a general handy man around the trading post and was perhaps twelve or thirteen years younger than Grandma Klah. His story began when he was five years old and his family and neighbors went to Fort Defiance and from there to the Bosque Redondo. He, with his mother, a younger sister, and a baby brother rode in a wagon all the way across the Pueblo country. When they came to the Río Grande, the horses were made to swim and tow the wagon like a boat, but when it was halfway across the current tipped it over and everybody went into the water. His mother held the baby, who was strapped to a cradleboard, on her head with one hand and clung to the wagon with the other. He and the smaller sister floated down the middle of the stream until a soldier on horseback caught him by one arm and lifted him onto his saddle. His sister was drowned. He could tell very little about the life at the Bosque or the return to his homeland, but he had much to tell about being captured by the Utes when he was ten or eleven years old and of being a slave boy for at least six years. He had been herding his mother's flock of sheep toward Rock Springs when a small party of Utes came riding swiftly from back of the mesa, grabbed him, and tied his hands and feet. They then watered their horses and turned north toward Ute Mountain, taking him with them. Six years later he stabbed his Ute owner and made his way back home.

Our third informant was a woman nearly as old as Grandma Klah who was known to us as Ahson Hoskay (Mad Woman). She was the matriarch of a large family and owned and managed a good-sized flock of sheep, and she could speak Spanish. As she lived some distance from the post, we interviewed her just the once and obtained only part of her story. She was one of the children who had never reached the Bosque Redondo, but had been stolen near the Isleta Pueblo. Her captors had sold her, with two or three other children, to a Jemez Indian who had traded them to a Mexican family for a number of sheep. In time she had married a Mexican, and they returned to her parents' home on the Río Chaco, where they accumulated wealth in the form of sheep and cattle.

The fourth on my list was Hosteen Allemigo's older wife, who said she was ten or eleven years old when they went on the Long Walk. Her parents took her to Fort Defiance when the government ordered all Navaho families to meet there before starting for the Bosque. They were quite prosperous and had a wagon, several horses, and a flock of sheep and goats which they took with them. But since they were one of the first families to reach the fort, they were forced to wait a whole year until the majority of their people could be rounded up and started on the long march. By this time

most of their sheep had been eaten or had died, as there
was not pasture for so many, and all of their horses but four
had been sold.

They were among the first in the long procession that
finally left Fort Defiance. After they had crossed the Río
Grande, a number of their group wished to go to the "Place
of Bells" (Albuquerque) to see the Mission Church. She
went with her mother and several other women, and a soldier was sent along to guard them. There were Mexican
farms all along the way, and, near an orchard, a dog frightened her horse so that it ran in among the trees and she
could not find her way out. A Mexican grabbed her bridle
and took her to his home. The soldier did not come after
her. Four years later, when the treaty had been signed and
the Navahos were allowed to return to their homeland, her
father collected all the beads, rings, and silver bracelets belonging to his clan to pay her ransom. When his group
reached Isleta, he hurried on ahead to locate the family
who owned her. This Mexican family lived just south of Albuquerque. Her father gave them all the jewelry he had
collected to buy her freedom; but they said it was not
enough, as Navaho women slaves were valued as high as
three hundred dollars. He waited until the whole group of
Navahos came, and then he added two horses to the payment. They had only two horses left, which were ridden by
her mother and an aunt, so she and her father walked during the journey home.

A very old man whom we called "Hosteen Escon," who
had never outgrown his bitterness against the government
and the soldiers, was next to tell his story of the Long Walk.
His family were not so well supplied with sheep and horses

as many of the others, and they were fewer in number. He was about twenty years old at the time and had a wife and one small child. They had one horse and a few sheep. His wife rode the horse and carried the baby, while he walked and herded the sheep. They had been told the government would give them food, but the rations were not sufficient to keep them alive. The only weapons they had were bows and arrows, and with these they killed rabbits, antelope, and prairie dogs to eat along the way. The soldiers were mean to them, and they were held like horses in big corrals so that they could not run away. While they were at the Bosque Redondo, they killed and ate their sheep, and then they had to go on raiding trips to steal food from the Puebloans in order to live, as the land they were given would not raise corn. The baby was the first to die, and then his brother and two of the brother's children died from eating spoiled meat the government had given them (pork). A year later his wife died in childbirth, and the baby was born dead. Only a few of his family survived.

When they were finally allowed to go back to their former homes, they stayed at Fort Wingate almost a year. When they did start for home, the Pueblo Indians were hostile all the way, and so were the Mexican ranchers. They both stole Navaho children to trade into slavery and also women when they could, as they wanted them for weavers. The Navahos retaliated by stealing children from the Puebloans. At Wingate the rations issued by the government were scanty and poor in quality, much of the food not fit to eat. Sometimes they would not have a meal for six or seven days, but would get along on piñones, cactus fruit, and spruce or pine buds. Their garments were made of buckskin or antelope hide, and the women wove their own squaw dresses and chief blankets for the men, but they did not sell any blankets.

From Fort Wingate they went to Fort Defiance, where better rations were provided and each Navaho was given two sheep, along with some farm tools for each family. Then they moved to the Chaco Valley, where they located and started a flock of sheep. They found wild horses in the Valley and caught all they needed for their own use. As soon as they had horses to ride, they raided the Pueblos north of Santa Fe and brought home many sheep and goats and also a few slaves. The soldiers came and told the slaves they were free to go home if they wished, but many preferred to stay, and Hosteen Escon's second wife was a girl from the Santa Clara Pueblo.

This was my last interview, for an epidemic of flu swept across the Reservation, taking a heavy toll of all the older people.

These records have been lying in my files for forty years, and now they provide an important part of the material I have used. Besides these writings, my main source of information was Hosteen Klah, whose excellent memory furnished me an inexhaustible supply of folklore, religious myth, and legend, as well as historical facts, names, and dates.

I have pleasant memories of long winter evenings before the huge open fireplace, sometimes with a baby in my lap or perhaps with my hands busy sewing some small garment while I listened to the deep voice of Hosteen Klah recounting traditions of his people or tribal events that took place long before he was born. Often he would pause to say,

"I may not be telling this again; why do you not write it down?" But generally there was something else I wished to do, and often I was weary at the close of day. Occasionally I did take my notebook and write for an hour or so when the events seemed more dramatic than usual, and now these pages furnish much of the material for this book. I certainly wish I had written much more.

The history of his people, as handed down orally through the generations, was a topic in which Hosteen Klah was well versed. Beginning with the small poverty-stricken bands of Navahos wandering from one river or mountain to another in search of small game animals, seeds, or nuts to maintain their precarious existence, he followed them through the many years when they were dependent on the Puebloans for corn and beans during the winters, often serving a term in slavery in return for food. These Navaho servants were not allowed to live in the pueblos or even inside the walls which encircled them, but built their temporary hogans in sheltered places near the fields where they worked.

From the Puebloans they gained their first knowledge of corn and soon learned to grind it and use the meal for food and for ceremonial purposes. In order to save the best corn for themselves the owners created a taboo that the Navahos must not touch any ears except the two small ones that grew at the very top of the cornstalk, and these were likely to be small nubbins. The other, larger ears were said to belong to the gods. The workers who herded the turkeys were warned not to kill a turkey or eat its flesh, as it would bring throat trouble and they would not be able to talk. To this day the Navahos refuse to eat the flesh of a turkey.

The Navaho tribe increased rapidly and soon spread out to places where they could have farms of their own with clan property rights. With the coming of the Spaniards, riding their hardy Spanish horses and accompanied by flocks of sheep and droves of cattle to furnish their food supply, the status of the Navahos was greatly changed. It did not take them long to realize the importance of owning horses and sheep, and soon they acquired both. Now they no longer begged food from the Puebloans, but demanded it.

A Navaho on foot was no menace to the Puebloans, but a Navaho or tribe of Navahos on horseback was a different equation. No longer were they a subservient race. They could strike, raid, and be away before the stone house dwellers could string their bows and shoot their arrows. The possession of horses brought a golden era of prosperity to the tribe. They stole sheep and goats from the Mexicans; from the Puebloans they stole corn and beans to plant in their own extensive fields, and wherever possible, they took women and children into slavery. The wealth of a clan was counted by the size of the flock of sheep, and for every man, woman, and child there was a horse to ride.

Klah invariably ended with a description of Navaho life as lived by his great-grandfather, the famous Chief Narbona, who at one time had commanded all the Navaho warriors on the eastern slope of the Chuska Mountains. It was by the number of horses he had counted his wealth. Narbona had many horses taken during many raids on different tribes, but there were only two he cared to ride. One was a beautiful Spanish palomino, and the other was the great roan stallion he had captured from the Utes. Realizing what an important place Narbona still occupied in the lives of Klah and his mother, I searched for historical records to add to Klah's story and have written the old Chief's story as Part I.

With this information I have attempted to outline the history of one family of Navaho Indians through four generations with some mention of the fifth and sixth, covering a period of almost two hundred years. Lucy Hapaha, my interpreter, was a member of the sixth generation. This family may have been typical of many other Navaho families living in other sections of the Southwest; at least many of the events described herein were experienced, not by this family alone, but by all the members of the Navaho nation.

In the last half of the eighteenth century, the population of that part of the Southwest lying between the Río Grande and the Colorado River was predominantly Indian. The greatest number of these native inhabitants were Puebloans who lived in walled villages or three-storied pueblos, near rivers or permanent springs, and depended on agriculture for their food supply.

To the north were the Utes, the Paiutes, the Arapahoes, and the San Carlos Apaches, all of whom were hunters sending out frequent war parties to raid neighboring tribes. In the south were the Mescalero Apaches, the Comanches, and the Mexicans. The semiarid central section was occupied by the Navahos. (See in this edition the map of Navaho country as made by Domínguez-Escalante Expedition in 1776.)

At that time a Spanish informant advised the Spanish governor that the Navaho tribe consisted of about 700 families numbering 3,500 people. The informant also stated that this tribe owned 500 horses, 600 wild mares, 700 black ewes (he does not list the white ones), 40 cows and their bulls, and many short-haired Mexican goats. Klah's estimate of the number of people and their stock did not agree with this in any detail excepting perhaps in the number of black ewes. He estimated around 1,200 families with twice as much livestock as the report listed.

These Navaho families were divided into five groups, living in widely separated territorial divisions. The division farthest west was located in and around the Canyon de Chelly; the second occupied a mountainous region south of Zuñi, which included Bear Springs (Fort Wingate) and a long section of the Río Puerco Valley. A small group were located at Cebolleta near the Laguna Pueblo, and a fourth of about the same size had their homes in or near the San Mateo Mountains around Mount Taylor. The fifth and by far the largest group occupied the eastern slopes of the To-hatchi, the Tunicha, and the Carrizo Mountains in the west and extended across the valleys and mesas to the Largo Canyon in the east. The diverse characteristics of this vast territory furnished the Indians with all the essentials necessary to create prosperity. The tree-covered mountains, which furnished wood for their hogans and fires and water from melting snows to irrigate their fields, were a pleasant abode during the hot summers and a safe refuge when enemies raided the lowlands. The wide, flat mesas covered with grama grass made excellent pastures for sheep and other livestock; and the fertile valleys, where lowlands were irrigated with little effort, became extensive fields in which corn, beans, squash, melons, pumpkins, and sometimes native tobacco were raised. The Navaho clans who had arrived in this section sometime before 1650 were augmented by fleeing Puebloans who wished to escape the persecution of the Spanish soldiers. These fugitives were made welcome by the Navahos, as they were fine pottery makers and possessed much knowledge of the use of medicinal herbs; and so a certain amount of Pueblo culture was transmitted to the Navahos along with one important healing rite, the Eagle Ceremony. From them the Navahos also learned to make adobe ovens in which to bake bread and roast meat. Up to this time, bread had been patted into flat cakes and baked on hot, flat stones while deer, antelope, and sheep were roasted over open pits. The Navahos called these newcomers the Myah (Coyote) Clan because, like the coyote, they had made their kill and then fled.

The battles between the Río Grande Puebloans and the Spanish invaders gave the Navaho raiding parties many opportunities to gather loose stock, loot corrals, and strip ripening fields. As they gained in wealth and numbers, they became more aggressive in their raiding and were greatly feared by the Mexican settlers and the more sedentary Puebloans. One of their main objectives was to obtain Pueblo girls and women, both as wives and to have pottery makers, as the Navaho women did not understand the art of making pottery.

Since the Navahos and the Apaches spoke nearly the same language and had the same living customs, they frequently formed alliances for raids and depredations against the common enemy. This greatly increased the Navaho area of operations, and there came a time when they could demand and receive tribute from the Spanish government. The leading chiefs of the Navaho tribe were given substantial bribes and in return halted their raids against the Spanish settlers. This truce was broken when Antonio, a prominent Navaho chief, was murdered. Later, a Spanish expedition under the leadership of Lieutenant Chacón massacred a number of Navaho women and children in Canyon del Muerto. From then on, the Navahos maintained a bitter enmity toward the Mexican and Spanish settlers and government which lasted for more than sixty years.

Albuquerque, New Mexico

FRANC JOHNSON NEWCOMB

Navaho vs. *Navajo*: Spellings of the names of Indian tribes frequently vary and thus present problems to both authors and publishers. In the case of Hosteen Klah's tribe, I, as a long-time resident of New Mexico, prefer the historical *Navajo*, which is used by the Navajo Tribal Council itself. The University of Oklahoma Press, like the Bureau of American Ethnology and many modern anthropologists, prefers *Navaho*. In this area I have bowed to my publisher's preference; therefore, except in direct quotations from published sources, *Navaho* it is in this book.—F. J. N.

xxvii

Acknowledgments and Thanks

To my daughter, Lynette E. Wilson, for faithful and expert typing which has made this volume possible.

To my friend, Lucy G. Bloomfield, who through the many years and at the present continues her interest in Indian welfare.

To my friend, Ellen Jones, for typing and assistance.

To Kenneth Foster, curator of the Museum of Navaho Ceremonial Arts, for photographs and data.

To Mr. Reed Mullen for a photograph of Klah's first sand-painting rug.

FRANC JOHNSON NEWCOMB

Contents

Illustrations

Map

PART ONE

Chief Narbona

1. Narbona Becomes Chief

As early as 1725 the Navaho nation had established its claim to vast areas of land in northern New Mexico and Arizona and in southern Colorado and Utah. They were not so powerful or warlike as the Comanches, Apaches, or Utes, and were never known to go into battle for the sole purpose of slaying their enemies. In fact, they avoided killing as much as possible because they did not wish to incur the wrath of enemy ghosts. But their young warriors were taught to be skillful raiders, the object of their raids being to obtain food or wealth in the form of sheep and horses.

For more than one hundred years the governors at Alcalde and Santa Fe were unable to halt or control these depredations. A letter written by Lieutenant Chacón, who was then in charge of territorial troops stationed at Alcalde, contains perhaps the first authentic description of the Navaho Indians of that period:

> The Navajos, whom we suspect have aided the Apaches in their invasions, have since the death of their leader, Dinnae-lhul-kish (Spotted Man), who met his death at the hands of an Apache, been irreconcilable enemies, to such a degree that with us they have observed an invariable and sincere peace. These Indians are not in a state of coveting flocks (sheep and goats), as their own are innumerable. They have increased their horse herds considerably; they sow much and on good fields; they work their wool with much more taste and delicacy than the Spaniards. Men as well as women go decently clothed, and their captains are rarely seen without silver jewelry.

This was doubtless a description of the Navahos living in the territory that included Bear Spring and the adjacent mountains, as Dinnae-lhul-kish was the outstanding chief of that area. His children and grandchildren claimed rights to this land as late as 1900, when it was purchased by the government. A great-grandson named "Pinto" was the last Navaho claimant.

This same description applied equally to the Navahos living along the eastern slopes of the Tunicha Mountains. They, too, were prosperous and industrious, rapidly increasing in numbers and in wealth. Clan groups, each numbering several families, generally owned large flocks of sheep which made necessary extensive pasture land and an unfailing water supply. Thus these groups could not live in communities but occupied widely separated areas and had no near neighbors.

Two of the more prominent clans claiming homesteads and grazing pastures of the eastern division were the Tzith-ah-ni, or "Brow-of-the-Mountain" clan, who were located on the Tunicha Mountains and claimed the lands of the Tunicha Valley; and the clan called "Yei-ee-dinnae," who lived in the Chuska Mountains and claimed the grazing land and water of the Tees-nas-pas Valley. Yei-ee-dinnae may not have been a clan name but may have indicated that one or more medicine men in their group were Yeibichai chanters. The majority of Navaho clan names were descriptive of some feature of the place they claimed as their homesites. For instance, the Des-cheeni clan are the people by the Red Rock Bend, and the Tsah-dish-kidi clan are those in the Sagebrush Hills.

Both of these groups were well situated and had acquired a large flock of sheep and herds of horses. Individual names of this older generation have been forgotten, but clan names are important. There is no law in the Navaho lexicon more rigidly observed than the law against clan intermarriage. Bi-kay-d-johl (Beads on her Shoes) was of the Tzith-ah-ni clan who were living at a place called Nee-yai-tsay, in the Tunicha Mountains. Narbona was born in the year 1766 to parents belonging to the Yei-ee-dinnae group living on the eastern slopes of the Chuska Mountains not far from the present trading post of Tsay-nas-tee. The parents of these two were fullblood Navahos, and the domain they claimed extended from the crest of the western mountains to the Río Chaco in the east. Included in this territory were fields that could be irrigated to raise corn, beans, squash, and melons; also there were mountain swales where tobacco and potatoes were grown. The rights to much of this land have been handed down through seven generations, so, at the present time, their descendants are grazing sheep on the same mesas and dipping water from the same springs as did their great-great-grandparents.

Narbona's childhood was, no doubt, spent in the same manner as that of all Navaho boys of that period. Until he reached the age of five he was considered a baby and was entirely under the care and protection of his mother and grandmother, who kept him near them at all times. In their hogans with open fireplaces and the outside primitive surroundings where snakes and an occasional bear were to be reckoned with, constant vigilance was necessary. When he reached the age of six, much of the responsibility for the boy's care and training was taken over by his father. He was given his own pony, which he soon learned to manage, and he rode with his father on short trips to the cornfields or to locate new pasture for the sheep.

At home his father devised exercises and games to develop his speed, strength, and agility. Every morning he and other boys of his age raced to a marker set at some distance and raced back again, the first to return earning applause. They practiced the broad jump, the throwing of round stones, and hurling the curved hunting stick in such manner that it would return to the thrower. When Narbona was twelve, he was given a bow and arrows made especially for him, the bow being exactly his own height. Now came real training toward becoming a skilled raider.

Since the economy of these Navaho families was entirely dependent on the whims of the spirits controlling the weather, they became accustomed to encountering one emergency after another and met even the worst with fortitude. However, in addition to natural calamities like blizzards which killed their sheep, grasshoppers which ate their corn, and drought which dried their streams, they lived in constant dread of raids by their enemies. They had built homes in the protection of the long wall of rugged mountains at the west; on the south the peaceful Puebloans were no threat. But to the north were the warlike Utes and Apaches, while some distance to the east were the Comanches. There was no mountain or water barrier to prevent these warriors from entering Navaho domain, and with these tribes there was never a truce. Raiding parties seem to have operated at will, capturing slaves, driving off livestock, killing men, and burning hogans to leave a trail of complete destruction in their wake.

By the age of fifteen nearly all Navaho boys were expert horsemen, excellent marksmen with the bow and arrow, and trained raiders. These youthful warriors must earn their standing in the tribe by successful forays into enemy territory to obtain horses and scalps.

There is no written history of this period of Navaho development, but members of the present generation repeat many tales of derring-do, of narrow escapes, and of grisly trophies exhibited at the war dances before the days of soldier domination. Long before his twentieth birthday, Narbona had earned the eagle feathers in his war bonnet and had captured his own trophies to exhibit at the "scalp dance." He was now the acknowledged leader of the youthful raiders, partly because of his skill in avoiding the enemy and partly because of his size. He was said to stand almost a head taller than the majority of his companions and to have the strength of a bear.

When Narbona was in his early twenties, his parents selected Bi-kay-d-johl of the Tzith-ah-ni clan to be his bride. Gifts were exchanged, and they were married with the Basket Ceremony. The young couple built their hogan in the Nee-yai-tsay glade not far from those occupied by her parents. Both young people had been given sheep as a start toward future wealth, and these, when added to the flocks of the parents, gave the family considerable prestige.

As the years passed, Narbona seems to have been very successful in his raids against the Mexicans and the neighboring Indians, acquiring much wealth in sheep and goats and also several slaves. His success caused many to enroll under his leadership, and he was recognized as the war chief of that section. He was the only Navaho war chief ever to command one thousand or more warriors.

7

By 1800, Bi-kay-d-johl's father was dead, and Narbona became the patriarch of the family. It is related that his family consisted of three wives, the second wife being a younger sister of his first wife, Bi-kay-d-johl, so their children were of the same clan. But the third was a girl from the Zuñi Pueblo, who may have been taken in a raid, but more likely was purchased with sheep and horses.

His wife's aged mother lived with them and helped care for almost a dozen children. The family owned more than two thousand sheep, two hundred Mexican goats, fifty head of cattle, and perhaps two hundred horses. The area required for grazing this amount of livestock was immense, and many helpers were needed to attend to their care. The sheep and goats were divided into medium-sized flocks with two or three herders in charge of each. Other herders were needed for the cattle and still others for the horses, which might stray too far from water and die of thirst or become mired in the adobe mud at the edge of a pond and perish. For this labor there were a few slaves, but these worked willingly, as there was nothing at all to keep them from running away and returning to their own tribe.

The majority of the helpers were recruited from the numerous indigent relatives and clan members who had no means or ability to support themselves and were glad to work for the headman, where they could be certain of safety, food, clothing, and shelter. There were also a number of orphans and aged persons belonging to their own clans or less fortunate groups who could not support them. This seems to have been the manner in which the headman of each section solved the problems of social security, orphanages, and homes for the aged. As far as the old people were concerned, it was a very satisfactory arrangement. They were still surrounded by the members of their own family and could contribute their bit to the general welfare.

Orphan children were taken into the family group, clothed, fed, and treated with the same care and love as the other children, but all were taught to work and do their share of the daily tasks. The older women carded and spun the yarn for blankets, gathered the materials for making dye, and cared for the babies and small children.

Two or three of the older couples lived in hogans at some distance from the main dwellings, and they were the silversmiths, leather tanners, moccasin makers, and saddle makers. After the men had made the buckskin garments, the women embroidered them with colored porcupine quills cut in short pieces like beads. All leatherwork was done by the men.

As each hogan had only one room, Narbona's large family necessitated several hogans, brush shelters, shepherd's huts, and corrals. In the home group there was a hogan for each of his wives, one for his mother-in-law, another for his married daughter, and one for his aunt. Dug into the bank of the nearby creek were two sweathouses, one bathhouse for the women and the other for the men. The main corral was backed into the wall of a projecting cliff and was enclosed on the other three sides by a high stone wall so that the animals were protected from the elements and also from hungry coyotes and bears. Several brush corrals were built conveniently near the best grazing areas, as it was not possible to bring the sheep home every evening.

The Navaho nation never was ruled by one central government, but each of the five divisions was headed by a chief who gained his title, not by inheritance, but by wisdom and ability. This chief was consulted on all matters of tribal or community interest and acted as delegate to all general council meetings. In the months of October and November, when the crops had been harvested, and the sheep and cattle were fat from the mountain pastures, the Navahos held their social gatherings.

Great religious ceremonials were held, during which their babies were named, their young people blessed, and the sick healed. When such a ceremony was planned, swift runners were dispatched to every place where Navahos were known to live, carrying to them invitations to the ceremony.

And they came! Over one thousand in number, dressed in their best fringed buckskins, beautifully woven blankets, red deer-hide shoes, and silver ornaments. At these major ceremonies there was generally one large hogan designated as a council house, and here the chiefs and leading men met to discuss tribal matters. Of these leaders of the five provinces, Narbona gradually took precedence. This may have been partly because of his wealth and the number of his followers, but more because of his success and ability as a great war chief.

2. *Defensive Strategy*

Sometime in the early 1820's a drought seared the Navaho country. How many years it lasted I do not know, but in the spring of the third year Narbona decided to move his family and the remainder of his flocks and herd to central Arizona, where he heard there was still water and grass. All of his ménage, his workers, and the majority of the Navahos living in his territory accompanied him on this trek. It must have been a difficult, tiresome journey, as sheep travel slowly and must be given time to graze along the way. We have no map of his route, but there was a halt in the Ganado Valley to allow the livestock to graze and the people to rest. Here one of his sons took a Navaho bride and was given a number of sheep and horses, as he wished to remain with his wife's family. (Miguelito, of Red Point, claimed to be a descendant of this couple and therefore Klah's cousin.)

The main safari continued westward into Hopi country, skirting the First, Second, and Third Mesas on which were the Hopi villages whose inhabitants were not exactly friendly to the Navahos. But the company was too large to attack, and there were no hostile demonstrations. Just beyond the Third Mesa they came to an enormously wide valley through the center of which flowed a good-sized stream. There may have been a few Navaho families living in this valley; at least there were no Hopi fields or flocks. Here Narbona established his domain. This wide valley still carries the name of Dinnae-bitoh-Wash (Navaho Water). At that time there were several large springs which gushed from the base of Third Mesa on the east and from Moenkopi Mesa on the west to furnish water for people, stock, grazing, and irrigation of extensive cornfields.

Just what arrangements Narbona made with the nearest Hopi chief is not known, but it is supposed that he paid with sheep and horses for rights to the land and so maintained friendly relations with these neighbors. During the eight or nine years this band of Navahos lived in Hopi territory, Narbona's children were growing into adults. Two of his sons and one daughter were married to Hopis. This daughter, Chay-endesbah, and her Hopi husband, Ahyahkini, were Klah's grandparents. These two lived with the Navaho group; the brothers who had married Hopi girls were given sheep and horses by their father and land holdings by the girls' father so they could settle by the Hopi village.

When Narbona heard that the rains and snows had returned to the Tunicha Mountains, he decided to return to his former home. All of his Navaho followers were delighted to be on their way to mountains where there were pine and spruce trees, cedar and piñon, as trees were few in the Arizona valley. The homeward journey was made in three weeks since there were not so many sheep or goats on this return trip and the party took a shorter route. They arrived at Nee-yai-tsay in time to start planting their fields, and the summer was spent in building new hogans, corrals, and dikes for the fields and in repairing the irrigation ditches. They extended their fields and built diversion dams of adobe, as they had acquired much useful knowledge about farming from their Hopi neighbors.

By autumn this group were comfortably established in their home territory, and, wishing to build back the flocks and herds they had lost during the drought, they started organized raids against the Mexican ranches lying in the fertile valleys north of Santa Fe. They took any sheep, goats, mules, cattle, or horses they could locate, and they kidnapped young women and children when they could do so without too much danger to themselves. Their greatest joy came when they were able to liberate a Navaho slave. The Mexican ranchers had many slaves from various tribes, but the Navahos worked the best and were considered the most valuable. Some of these were satisfied with the treatment they received at the hands of their captors and refused to return to their own tribe; they were termed "Enemy Navaho." For many years the history of New Mexico is a record of Navaho raids against all pueblos and ranches; government encouragement of forays and expeditions into Navaho territory; groups of Navahos betrayed and slaughtered by Mexicans, Jicarillas, and Taos; and treaties made and broken by both sides.

In the fall of 1835, many Mexican ranchers and a troop of soldiers under the command of Captain Hinófos decided to march into Navaho country, destroy their fields, kill or scatter their flocks, burn their hogans, and shoot as many of their people as they could find. There were more than three hundred in this corps, since most of the leading men of northern New Mexico joined the expedition. They did not expect the least resistance from the Navaho Indians, who were thought to be divided into small groups of raiders who could never make a stand against such a large force. But they reckoned without Chief Narbona.

As this was harvest season, with most of the corn, beans, melons, and squash still ripening in the fields, it would mean

13

starvation for many Navaho families if three or four hundred horses and mules trampled the crops underfoot. Having been informed of the approach of this war party while it was still in the Jemez Mountains, where the corps had reached the headwaters of the Río Chaco and were following this stream in order to be assured of water for horses and men, Narbona had time to collect his warriors and prepare a surprise defense.

Chief Narbona assembled two hundred warriors, most of them young men who were eager to earn honors in battle. A few of them carried muskets, but the majority were armed with their long war bows and iron-tipped arrows. (In the Museum of Navaho Ceremonial Arts in Santa Fe, there is a war bow and arrows that were probably carried by a Navaho warrior in this affair.) All the Navahos were mounted bareback on their swiftest horses, and many had painted their faces with red ocher. Since in order for the arrows to be effective, the marksmen must come to fairly close quarters with the enemy, an ambuscade was planned at the Big Bend of the Río Chaco. Here a high headland of sandstone hid the warriors until the approaching raiders turned the bend and were almost upon them. For an account of this affair, I quote from Josiah Gregg's *Commerce of the Prairies* (Chapter 15, "Wild Tribes of New Mexico"):

> The valiant corps, utterly unconscious of the reception that awaited them, soon came jogging along in scattered groups, indulging in every kind of boisterous mirth; when the warwhoop, loud and shrill, followed by several shots, threw them all into a state of speechless consternation. Some tumbled off their horses with fright, others fired their muskets at random; a terrific panic had seized everybody, and some minutes

elapsed before they could recover their senses sufficiently to betake themselves to their heels. Two or three persons were killed in this ridiculous engagement, the most conspicuous of whom was Capt. Hinófos, who commanded the regular troops.

This victory was almost too easy to suit many of the younger Navaho warriors, who were eager to pursue the retreating army and gather a few scalps. But Narbona refused to allow further pursuit, for he well knew the superior number of guns might reverse the victory if the Mexicans made a firm stand. The Mexican raiders were allowed to retreat, taking their dead and wounded with them.

The young warriors were also disappointed in the animals they had captured, as the greater number were old, rawboned army mules—discards from the troops stationed near Santa Fe which this expedition had used as pack animals. The few horses they captured were highly prized, but, as my informant stated, the mules were so old and tough they would hardly make good stew meat. However, there is little the Navahos do not put to some use, and mule hides furnish the toughest leather for making saddles and drums. There was still a goodly bit of loot to be divided since the packs on the mules contained more than half the supplies the corps had started with. There were blankets, canteens, food supplies, powder and shot, and even an occasional musket still held in the gun-boot strapped to a saddle.

It was a wildly hilarious cavalcade of Navahos who returned to their homes in the Tunicha Valley, driving the captured horses and mules and shouting defiance to all enemies of the Navaho tribe. The members of the invading army returned to their homes quite disheartened to tell of being beset by thousands of painted warriors and barely escaping with their lives. No more expeditions were sent into the Navaho country from that direction until United States soldiers were stationed at Santa Fe.

In the Tunicha Valley a war ceremonial was organized as soon as possible in which each warrior, young or old, enacted his own glorious part in the successful encounter. Navahos came from far and wide to attend this war dance, and news of the victory spread to every corner of the Navaho territory and also to the Pueblo villages and Mexican haciendas. Narbona's name brought fear to his enemies, but more and more Navaho families came to live on the eastern slopes of the Chuska Mountains and swell the number of his followers. The young warriors, believing themselves invincible, raided in all directions until every pueblo and every *ranchería* became a fortress with all their inhabitants fearing and hating the Navahos.

When the corn was ripe in the fall and the summer rains had filled the arroyos and water holes, the ceremonial season began. Now the sheep were fat and food was plentiful. The Navahos gathered around evening fires near the fields where, during the day, they had been busy husking corn, flailing beans, and cutting squash and pumpkins into long strips to dry in the clear autumn air. Boys and young men formed a circle surrounding a drummer and rehearsed the plaintive chants they would sing at the next Yeibichai. Everyone would have been very happy and content if it had not been for the ever present threat of raiders. This harvesting activity was well known to the enemy tribes on the north and east. If they could send raiding parties to catch the Navahos unawares, they could capture many slaves and horses.

As the lowlands of the Tunicha Valley were now widely cultivated, they became the main target of raiders from these two directions. About six or seven miles north of this area there rises a large mass of volcanic rock which the Navahos call Tsis-nah-jin (Black Rock). The name on the map is Bennett Peak. From the top of this the lower country can be scanned for many miles in every direction. To the southeast a red butte rears its crest high above the surrounding land. On these high points, Narbona stationed watchers to flash smoke signals by day or fire flashes at night to warn the workers in the fields of approaching enemies. This gave Narbona time in which to gather a formidable war troop, arrange an ambush, and pretty well annihilate the raiders. After a few disastrous forays, the Utes and Apaches decided to turn their efforts toward other Navaho communities, and the Tunicha Valley was left in peace.

There is one tale of a Comanche war party that followed the San Juan River until they came to the mouth of the Río Chaco, where they turned south into the Navaho country. The Comanches were excellent horsemen and owned beautiful horses, the envy of all Navaho riders. This band of raiders numbered about twenty young Indians led by the son of their chieftain, all mounted on their fleetest ponies. Again the Navahos were warned of approaching enemies and planned an ambush many miles down the valley where it would least be expected. In this encounter more than half the Comanches were killed and the remainder fled, leaving their dead behind, taking only the body of the chief's son.

Among the horses captured by the Navahos was a beautiful roan stallion that had been ridden by the chieftain's son, and this horse Narbona claimed as his prize. It is remembered as being a large horse of a light roan color with brownish spots on its rump and shoulders. It was probably the first Appaloosa ever owned by a Navaho.

3. Lords of the Soil

As THE YEARS PASSED, the Navaho tribe made great gains in numbers and in wealth. They came to regard the neighboring Puebloans as vassals who were obliged to contribute to their support. This attitude is well expressed in a paragraph from *A Short History of the Navajo People,* by Richard Van Valkenburgh:

> In 1837 the Navajo had become a scourge, raiding and plundering both Mexican and Puebloan villages at will. They were well on their way to destroy completely the settlements on the Rio Grande. These "Lords of the Soil," as they were called in those days, boldly stated that they did not care to steal the breeding ewes as then there would be no lambs to steal in the spring. In this atmosphere of plunder and depredation, Nahabaahi (Narbona) was the outstanding Navajo leader. Klee-thlunie (Many Horses) and Manuelito, who was Narbona's son-in-law, were young men at the time and skilled warriors.

Chee Dodge, who was chief of the Navahos for many years, relates incidents in the life of his grandfather, a prominent man who owned many slaves:

> My grandfather had slaves to do all of the outside work such as caring for the sheep, herding the horses, and harvesting the crops. He even had a personal slave who was always handy to saddle his horse if he wished to ride and unsaddle when he returned; to spread the buffalo robes he used for bedding at night and to take them out in the sun in the morning; and to run whatever errands he was assigned.

Just as the Puebloans were considered an asset to Navaho economy, so were the Spanish and Mexican settlers who were now establishing homes along the Río Grande. Their settlements did not encroach on Navaho territory or threaten their rights in any way, and they did supply a certain amount of trade goods through either barter or hit-and-run raids. Their farms and irrigation projects were not molested, for, as one Navaho leader said, "We can help ourselves to their harvest in the fall, so why not let them raise all the corn they can." Naturally these settlers became bitter enemies of the Navahos.[1]

But life among the Navaho clans was not all given to labor, strife, and raiding; there were also many social and religious activities. Although these people lived in isolated clan groups and had no villages or community centers, they still maintained intimate contact through harvest festivals, war dances, and healing ceremonies. As all such gatherings of any kind or purpose were religious in character, the medicine man was the arbiter and master of ceremonies for each occasion and was given complete authority in the arrangement of the elaborate ritual and ceremony.

During the early days of Navaho life in the Southwest, these people had been in contact with the people of the great pueblos which now lie in ruins along the rivers and streams.

---

[1] It was during this period that the residents of the four Pueblos nearest Navaho territory, namely, the Laguna, the Isleta, the Jemez, and the San Ildefonso Indians, started a custom which has continued to the present time. They made an agreement with the Navahos whereby their fields were not to be touched during planting or growing season; then, when the crops were harvested and the Puebloans were celebrating their harvest festivals, the Navahos could come and they would be given all the corn, squash, beans, and melons they could carry away. Hundreds of Navahos still attend these fall festivals, and wagonloads of farm produce are given them by the Puebloans.

From these "Anat-sazi" (Old Ones) the Navahos learned rites, prayers, and chants which they adopted and to which they added ceremonial procedure, thus forming a complex of ceremonialism that grew through the passing years. When prosperity was finally achieved, Navaho religious ceremonials reached the zenith of intricacy and continued at this magnitude until the time of United States military domination, when insecurity and loss of wealth brought a drastic change. Although religious festivals were still held, the number of days was shortened, and they were hidden in rough mountain terrain where strangers would not find them. Another curtailment was in the number of guests invited.

At the height of ceremonial activity some of the principal ceremonies were the Water Chant, the Rain Dance, the Hail Chant, the Wind Rites, the Shooting Chant, the Mountain Chant, and several others, all of which lasted nine days and nights. Then there were war dances, peace festivals, and harvest ceremonies which lasted five days and nights. Most of these ceremonies were held after the harvest since hundreds of visitors attended and there must be food for all, as well as water and pasture for the horses they rode.

During the daytime there were amusements for young and old; for the young men there were games to test their strength and skill in running, jumping, archery, and horse racing; for the older guests there were gambling games with round stones, with flat, colored sticks, or with wooden dice; and for everyone there was feasting. The games and the cooking halted only when some short religious rite outside the ceremonial lodge was in progress. At night bonfires were lighted around which the young men gathered to practice the songs they would sing when they joined the masked dancers on the last night, while in the ceremonial lodge the medicine man and his group of neophytes chanted prayers, interspersed with rites of exorcism, from darkness to dawn.

The Navahos never did think of themselves as a conquered race, either by the Spaniards or by the Mexicans. They thought of themselves as constituting a free nation living on its own ancestral land, supporting its own economy, and ably repelling its enemies. They asked no assistance and certainly received none from either of these two regimes. They had gained their present status of independence with the arrival of the Spaniards in the Southwest and the acquisition of horses and sheep, but had never felt the iron heel of governmental authority. Because of the desert terrain, the extent of territory, and unapproachable mountain vastnesses, the punitive expeditions sent by the Spaniards against the Navahos had met with little success.

Between 1822 and 1846, a period of twenty-four years of Mexican rule, the new government decided that it would be easier to pay tribute to the Navahos than to fight them and would cost much less. Navaho independence lasted until a few years after General Kearny captured Santa Fe and took possession of the territory of New Mexico in the name of the United States of America.

As soon as the new government was established, it was besieged with complaints and accusations against the Navaho Indians. Traders, stockmen, ranchers, and Puebloans brought in such a mass of indictments that the governor decided something must be done about these depredations. Friendly Navahos from the Cebolleta group were sent to all parts of the Navaho country requesting the chiefs and leaders to come to Santa Fe to pledge their loyalty to the new government and to sign a treaty of peace. Former governors had sent out similar requests but, on two occasions, had not been able to prevent the hostile Puebloans from murdering the Navaho delegates who attended. This treachery was greatly resented by the Navaho tribe, and so Narbona did not go, but sent word to the governor that any treaty he and his councilors signed would have to be executed on Navaho territory. To this the governor agreed.

So many tales of the new government and the activities of its troops were spreading through Navaho country that, in the late summer of 1846, Narbona decided to travel to Santa Fe to obtain firsthand information concerning Fort Marcy, the soldiers, and the new regime he was hearing so much about. His followers tried to dissuade him from taking this trip, as they were afraid he would be captured and held as hostage or perhaps killed outright, leaving them without a leader. Since he, too, was fearful of what might happen if the soldiers or the Mexican settlers knew he was there, he took with him only a few of his older councilors and traveled at night. They did not use the Jemez Mountain Pass, but rode far to the north and crossed the mountains by a deer trail known only to a few hunters. Approaching Santa Fe from the north, they made no attempt to enter the compound of Fort Marcy or the streets leading to the city of Santa Fe, but remained safely hidden in the surrounding hills where they could view the activities of the fort and the city without being discovered.

They did have one or two narrow escapes from being reported to the governor. Once, when two of their number were watering their horses at a creek, six Tesuque Indians came riding by and demanded to know who they were. One of the Navahos could speak their language and replied, "We are Navahos from Cebolleta and we are on our way to see the governor, who has sent for us." This explanation satisfied the Tesuques, as they knew the Cebolleta Navahos were often used by the new government as messengers. And again the next morning when they had packed everything on their horses and had ridden some distance from their camping place, keeping below the crest of the hills, they saw a party of soldiers ride up and examine the remains of their campfire. One soldier dismounted and kicked the ashes, which were probably still warm. The Navahos quickly urged their horses into a gully and rode away, keeping behind the hills. The next night they divided and found hiding places two by two. The next morning all traces of their stay were obliterated, and they started for home.

This new Fort Marcy, with its regimental drills, its cavalry parades, and its thundering cannon, was a force the Navahos had never imagined could exist. On the homeward ride they all agreed that Navaho warriors could never win against these troops and that it would be well to establish friendship with the Americans. After his return from Santa Fe, Narbona called many council meetings to discuss government orders and decide on a future course of action. The older councilmen advised a cessation of hostile activities against the Río Grande settlers and the Puebloans to the east, even though war with the Utes and Apaches still continued. The younger members did not agree with this plan, as the settlers were their main source of livelihood. The older men were well fixed, with large flocks of sheep and herds of horses, but the younger men were not so well provided for and resented the curtailment of their activities.

As these young men were a large majority, little attention was paid to the advice given by Narbona. Without his
knowledge or consent, they formed into raiding parties
which ranged the country as far north as Taos, east to the
Río Grande, and south to the Sacramento Mountains.
Whether they ever waylaid and ravaged caravans on the
Santa Fe Trail is a matter of debate, as there were few
white people at that time who could tell the difference between a Navaho and an Apache, but many of the "wagon
massacres" were laid to their door. In *Commerce of the Prairies*, Gregg quotes old trappers as saying they feared the
Kiowas and the Apaches, but they were safe when they
reached the land of the Navahos.

In late winter of 1846, a military expedition under the
leadership of Lieutenant Doniphan, with 350 soldiers of
the First Regiment of Missouri Volunteers, marched into
Navaho territory. They passed through Cubero, over the
Continental Divide at Thoreau, and thence down the Río
Gallo to meet with more than a thousand Navahos at Ojo
del Oso (Bear Springs), later the site of Fort Wingate. A
council was held and the "Treaty of Bear Springs" was written by Lieutenant Doniphan and signed by fifteen Navaho
chieftains, the most important of whom were Narbona, Zar-
zilla (Long Earrings), and José Largo. In order to attend
this council meeting, Narbona, who was then eighty years
old and suffering from a severe attack of influenza, was
brought to Bear Springs in a litter swung between two
horses. Klah has been told that this epidemic caused many
deaths among the Navahos and believes it to be of the same
character as the epidemics of 1919.

This first treaty with the Americans was kept only

through the winter and early spring; with warm weather, raiding was again a major occupation of the "wild tribes." Between the signing of the treaty at Bear Springs and the autumn of 1849, no less than five military expeditions of United States troops took the field against the Navahos. All were unsuccessful. Even though the Navahos were able to avoid contact with the soldiers carrying out these forays, they began to feel the effects of these incursions severely. They were rapidly losing the greater number of their sheep and horses, the crops in the fields were destroyed before they could be harvested, and they were forced to live in hidden canyons and mountain fastnesses.

A certain part of this destruction could be laid to the enmity of the Puebloans, who saw in the soldiers an opportunity to avenge themselves for losses they had sustained at the hands of the Navahos. They were glad to act as guides for the expeditions into Navaho territory and to point out the farms and grazing areas where livestock might be found. They also had some knowledge of the hidden canyons and rock escarpments where Navaho homes were often located. But the Puebloans found this campaign of hate highly retroactive. As the Navahos lost their livestock and were stripped of their harvests of corn and beans, they were obliged to depend more and more on their Pueblo neighbors for their food supply. No more was this a matter of feeding a few hungry Navaho families who were willing to work in the fields for a ration of corn and mutton. It was now a hungry horde numbering well into the thousands who were ready to kill to obtain food and horses.

Two or three dry summers during the time of harassment added a shortage of water to plague the Navaho farmers and shepherds. They began to wonder why their gods had turned against them and in what manner they had failed to please them. One Blind Prophet dreamed that all Navaho people would perish and a new race would occupy their land. Many ceremonies were held, and gifts were carried to high places and laid on altars to appease the gods. Finally it was decided that four medicine men would make the journey to Tohe-ha-glee (Meeting Place of Waters) and scan the "Page of Prophecy" for an answer to their questionings.

For this trip they chose the oldest and wisest medicine men, each from a different part of the Navaho country, and instructed them to meet at Black Rock to make their preparations. The whole Navaho nation started a period of prayer while the four chanters were going through purification rites, prayer ceremonies, and days and nights of fasting. They must put themselves on a higher plane than ordinary mortals before they could expect to receive any communication from gods who made their home on Tse-thanie-tsa.

Five of the most important members of the Navaho pantheon of immortals were said to make their homes on the high rock called Tse-thanie-tsa, which overlooked the Shining Sands of Prophecy. There was a legend of a visit from these gods, who, when they returned to their homes, left a trail which only holy ones might follow. So accurate was the description that these four shamans could follow almost in the gods' footsteps. Each man wore only ceremonial clothing with a sacred buckskin for a blanket and carried sacred cornmeal in a prehistoric pottery bowl.

They reached the bank of the river late in the afternoon and gathered four kinds of wood from the four directions. With the whirling stick they made a small fire and ate their mush before darkness descended. All night long they squatted by their fire and chanted prayers of supplication to the immortals, while at home all the medicine men with their families were chanting the same prayers:

> *May the way be blessed before us,*
> *May the way be blessed behind us,*
> *May the sky be glorious above us,*
> *May the earth be fruitful around us.*

In the morning they approached the face of the cliff and, finding a flat ledge high up on one side, placed their gifts of turquoise, white shell, red coral, yellow pollen, and black jet where the gods would find them, then made their way to the Shining Sands. Where the rivers met, there was an expanse of bright sand thinly covered with slowly moving water. The message the gods had written for them through the night would be drawn in symbolic design in the sand under the water.

For a time the four gazed silently at the Page of Prophecy, so as not to miss any part of the message that had been written for them. After a while, they began pointing out different marks and designs and discussing their meanings. There were long straight marks that resembled reeds, and they took these as signs of heavy rains; there was a deep groove in the sand that went beyond the water's edge and was lost in the grasses which seemed to be marked with footprints at intervals. This was thought to be a journey to a distant place. There were wavy lines that told of wind and lightning and floods, there were stalks of corn and wheat that prophesied good crops, and there were many straight marks crossing each other in the manner of the crossed sticks that mark a burial. It was not a happy four who returned to their homes to report the messages they had read from the Page of Prophecy.[2]

[2] To my knowledge there have been two more journeys made to the "Shining Sands" to read the "Page of Prophecy." One was in 1868 when the Navahos first came home from the Bosque Redondo and were in a state of semistarvation, and the other was in 1929 when they were facing starvation after the commissioner of Indian Affairs had ordered the killing of most of the horses and goats and a great reduction in the number of sheep each family was allowed to own.

29

4. The Death of Narbona

BETWEEN 1846 and 1849, the Bear Springs Treaty had been broken continuously by both the Navahos and the Apaches. Five more military expeditions of United States soldiers had been sent against the Navahos, and two more treaties had been signed, both of which proved to be useless scraps of paper. These troops carried out a "scorched-earth" policy wherever they crossed Navaho territory, killing livestock, trampling fields, and burning hogans. Although they seldom came into contact with the Navaho people, they succeeded in wrecking their economy wherever they marched. The Navaho families in thickly settled areas began to scatter to find homes beyond the periphery of the military invasions. Some went past El Huerfano Peaks, which served as a protective barrier; others went into Colorado as far as Mesa Verde to live in La Plata Mountains.

The canyons of Arizona as far west as the Grand Canyon were now occupied by various Navaho clans, who brought their livestock with them for the purpose of establishing permanent homes where there was safety and freedom. The Canyon de Chelly, with its many branching canyons and its unfailing flow of water, sheltered more than five hundred families. And so the Navaho tribe, with widely separated communities, extended its territory to the north and the west, more than double its former extent.

Narbona, his family, and his followers did not flee to new territory, but continued to live on the eastern slopes of the Tunicha, the Tohatchi, and the Carrizo Mountains. However, their homes were no longer built in open glades or near wide fields. Higher in the mountains there were rocky ridges where they felt secure, and all homes on the lower slopes were hidden in the canyons or so surrounded by brush as to resemble part of the landscape. This became an established practice, and even many years later strangers could cross the Reservation and not discover a single Navaho dwelling. Horses were pastured in mountain swales, while sheep and goats climbed the higher slopes. So the Navahos managed to live, but it was not the carefree existence of former years.

Narbona called many council meetings and advised his headmen and his followers to send word to the governor in Santa Fe that all the Navahos on this side of the mountains desired peace and would agree to whatever terms were offered to establish friendship. He suggested sending a delegation to deliver this message, but his followers voiced many objections. First, they were certain that any small group trying to cross Pueblo territory would be caught and massacred on the way;[3] and second, the governor was sure to put

[3] For some time, the territorial governors had been offering a bounty of ten dollars for each coyote, Apache, or Navaho scalp that was brought to their offices. This offer attracted many old Indian fighters, so-called "mountain men," and trappers to the Southwest, where they were generally known as "scalp hunters." These men dared not venture far into Apache or Navaho territory, but they did scout all mountain and valley trails and maintained watch at all watering places to waylay small groups of Indians traveling outside their own domain. Most of the "scalp massacres" that are still remembered took place near some spring or small stream where the Indians' ponies were being watered.

Scalp hunting became such a lucrative occupation that many renegade whites took it up and killed anyone, man, woman, or child, who happened to have black hair. This included the Mexicans, Spanish, Puebloans, Comanches, Utes, and some whites. On the overland trails the caravans were not safe without armed escorts, and most of them

them in prison where they would be held for weeks or months until he could obtain verification of their message. The third reason was the most important and really insurmountable—the governor had demanded the return of all slaves and livestock the Navahos had stolen from either the Mexicans or the Puebloans before any treaty of friendship with the Navahos could be made. Seizing this golden opportunity for revenge, the latter had piled the governor's desk with lists of missing sheep, goats, cattle, and horses in which were included all that had been stolen by the Apaches, the Comanches, and the Utes.

Narbona well knew that the surrender of this amount of livestock would leave the Navahos stripped to the point of starvation, and to this he would not agree.

He was now eighty-three years old, and although his older followers regarded him as the wisest of all leaders, many of the younger warriors refused to listen to his counsel. One of these was his son-in-law, Manuelito, who was gaining control of a rebellious band of young braves who held their own council meetings and planned their own raids into enemy territory. Thus the eastern Navahos became divided in their allegiance, some approving the tactics of the rebellious young men and others fearful of the results.

At this time there was a blind prophet living on the west side of the mountain. Since he had been blind from birth, his name was Binah-uhtin, and he was said to "see with his mind." As the years passed, his dreams, or perhaps just his thoughts, came to be considered prophecies of coming

---

asked for troop protection. Many of the massacres said to have been done by the Apaches were really committed by these renegades.

The bounty for scalps was finally withdrawn, and several of the scalp hunters joined the U.S. troops as army scouts.

events. Binah-uhtin came to the eastern side of the mountains to attend a War Chant (now known as Squaw Dances) and came into contact with some of the young braves. He told these young warriors that they were doing wrong in not heeding the council of the older chiefs, that they were young and foolish and could think no farther than the present day. He said, "The day will come when your enemies will drive you out of your homeland, and you will go to a barren country where the corn will not grow and your sheep will eat poison weeds and die. Many of your people will starve, and others will be killed so that only a few will survive, and in all these wide cornfields there will be nothing alive excepting the coyotes and the crows."

Many were inclined to believe this prediction, but its fulfillment seemed a long time in the future, and right now there were enemies to be dealt with. For thirteen more years the Navahos made war on the surrounding tribes, and everyone made war on the Navahos.

In August of 1849, Lieutenant Colonel John Washington, military commander of the territory of New Mexico, led an expedition against the Navahos. Besides the officers and staff, there was a cavalry troop of 175 members and a group of 250 New Mexicans, all well mounted and armed. This army of invasion was guided by a Cebolleta Navaho named Sandoval and by a couple of Jemez Indians. Army mules pulling two cannon and many wagons of supplies brought up the rear. Crossing the Jemez Mountains, this cavalcade followed the Río Chaco, which supplied them with water.

They paused two days in Chaco Canyon to explore the prehistoric ruins, and Lieutenant Simpson wrote good descriptions of Pueblo Bonito and Chetro Kettle.

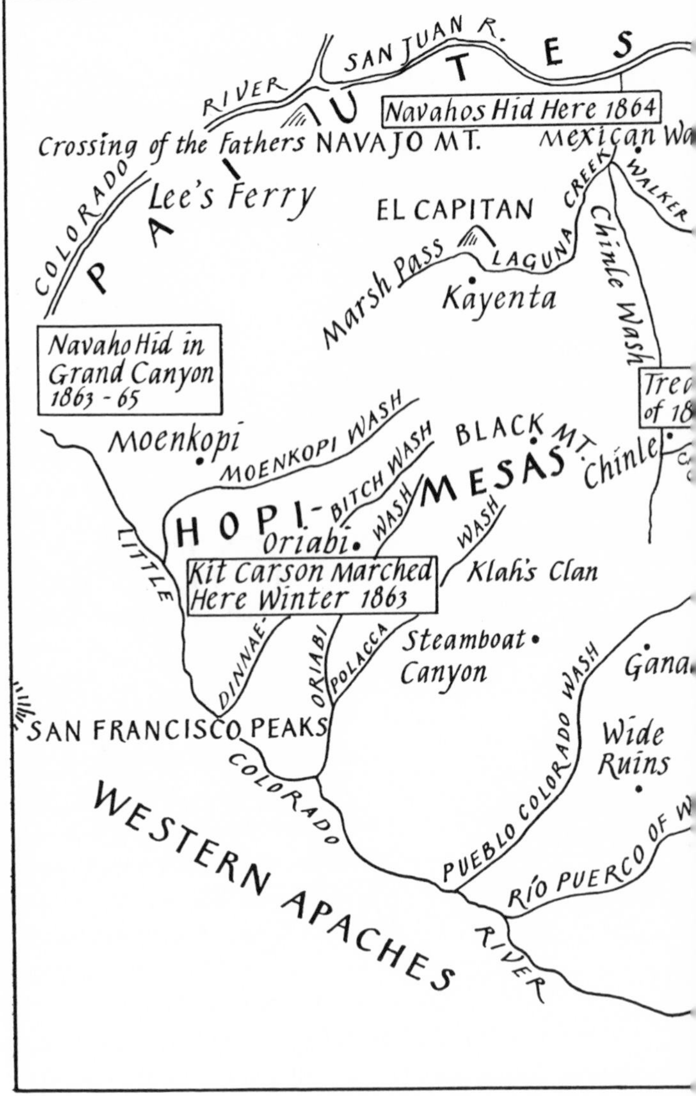

SAN JUAN R.
RIVER
COLORADO
P A I U T E S
Navahos Hid Here 1864
Crossing of the Fathers
NAVAJO MT.
Mexican Wa
WALKER
Lee's Ferry
EL CAPITAN
LAGUNA CREEK
Chinle Wash
Marsh Pass
Kayenta
Navaho Hid in Grand Canyon 1863 - 65
Tre
of 18
Moenkopi
MOENKOPI WASH
BITCH WASH
BLACK MT.
HOPI MESAS
Chinle
WASH
WASH
Oriabi
LITTLE
Kit Carson Marched Here Winter 1863
Klah's Clan
DINNAE
ORIABI
POLACCA
Steamboat Canyon
PUEBLO COLORADO WASH
Gana
Wide Ruins
SAN FRANCISCO PEAKS
COLORADO
WESTERN APACHES
PUEBLO
RÍO PUERCO OF W
RIVER

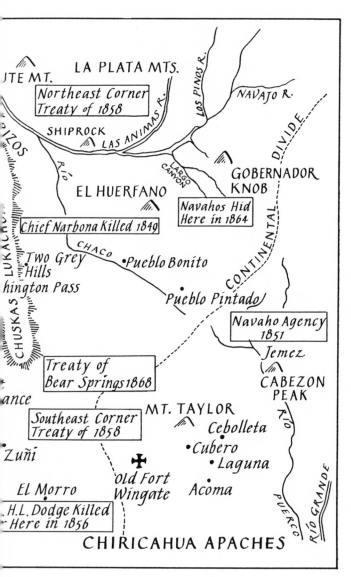

NAVAHO COUNTRY, 1846–68

The Navahos of the eastern division were dismayed at the size of this army and the speed at which they were approaching. Families were then living in their fields, and the crops had not been harvested. Narbona collected fifteen horses, ten mules, and about fifty sheep to deliver to the soldiers with the request that the commander avoid the Naschiti cornfields where the hogans were located. Colonel Washington replied that he could not do so, as his horses and mules must feed on the cornfields. So the Navaho families gathered all the food they could carry, packed their possessions on their horses, and fled to the mountains.

The troops left the Río Chaco at the Big Bend and marched to the Tunicha Valley, destroying all the cornfields along their way, and always aware that hidden Navahos were keeping watch on their progress. Narbona had received reports from the army scouts informing him of the purpose and the destination of the troops. When he heard that the council meeting would be held on the western side of the mountains at the mouth of Canyon de Chelly, he decided he could not attend in person. He conferred with Chief José Largo, who was also quite old and infirm, and they decided to ask for a meeting with Colonel Washington, suggesting the names of two younger Navaho leaders to act as their proxies.

Wishing to appear before the white commander in the dignified role of a great Navaho chief, Narbona called together the majority of the Navaho men in his section, who may have numbered about eight hundred warriors. A smaller group was sent on ahead, driving one thousand sheep and a few head of cattle in obedience to the demand that all stolen livestock must be returned. Three of the younger chiefs asked to be given an interview with Colonel Washington and Mr. James Calhoun, superintendent of Indian affairs, to find out exactly what the government wished the Navahos to do. This delegation was informed that if they did not comply with the terms of the Nuby Treaty (Bear Springs) and give up all Mexican captives, all murderers of Mexicans who had found sanctuary among them, and all Mexican livestock, a body of troops would be sent to enforce their doing so. These two Navahos promised to send word to all other chiefs to be in camp tomorrow at noon and have these matters settled.

The next day, August 31, 1849, Narbona and his men rode to the guard lines of the army camp, where the main body halted and Narbona with his headmen were escorted to the tent of Colonel Washington. The Simpson report describes Narbona in these words: "Another man who was quite old and of very large frame, had a grave and contemplative countenance not unlike (as many of the officers remarked) that of General Washington. He wore a striped, hand-woven blanket over his shoulders." To this group, Calhoun proceeded to explain the terms of the treaty, with Mr. Conkling as interpreter. Lieutenant Simpson gives us a detailed report of this conference, held between the government officials and the three elderly Navaho chieftains—Narbona, José Largo, and Archuletta.

> *Mr. Calhoun*: Tell them they are lawfully in the jurisdiction of the United States, and they must respect that jurisdiction.
> *Interpreter*: They say they understand it.
> *Mr. Calhoun*: Tell them that after the treaty is made, their friends will be the friends of the United States, and their enemies the enemies of the United States.

37

Tell them when any difficulty occurs between them and any other nation, by appealing to the United States they may get redress.

Are they willing to be at peace with all the friends of the United States?

Interpreter: They say they are willing.

Mr. Calhoun: Tell them that by the treaty which it is proposed to make with them, all trade between themselves and other nations will be recognized as under regulations to be prescribed by the United States.

Colonel Washington: And the object of this is to prevent their being imposed upon by bad men.

Interpreter: They understand it, and are content.

Mr. Calhoun: Tell them if any wrong is done them by a citizen of the United States, or by a Mexican, he or they shall be punished by the United States, as if the wrong had been done by a citizen of the United States, and on a citizen of the United States.

Interpreter: They say they understand it, and it is all right.

Mr. Calhoun: That the people of the United States shall go in and out of their country without molestation, under such regulations as shall be prescribed by the United States.

Interpreter: They say they will.

Mr. Calhoun: Tell them that, by this treaty, the government of the United States are to be recognized as having the right to establish military posts in their country wherever they may think it necessary, in order to [assure] the protection of them and their rights.

That the government of the United States claim the right to have their boundaries fixed and marked, so as to prevent any misunderstanding on this point between them and their neighbors.

Interpreter: They say they are very glad.

Mr. Calhoun: For and in consideration of all this, and a faithful performance of the treaty, the government of the

United States will, from time to time, make them presents, such as axes, hoes, and other farming utensils, blankets, etc.
Interpreter: They say it is all right.

After all nine points of the treaty had been explained to the chiefs and other headmen in attendance and they had indicated their approval, Narbona and José Largo expressed their wish to be excused from attending the council at De Chelly, stating that they would send delegates to take their places. Papers were signed giving powers of attorney to Armijo and Pedro José, both of whom spoke enough Spanish to make themselves understood. These two younger chiefs now had authority to act for them at the De Chelly council, in the same manner and to the same extent as if they were present.

The council having ended, the group of Navahos walked back to their tribesmen and mounted their horses. It was a colorful spectacle: all wore red, yellow, or blue striped blankets and some wore helmets topped by eagle feathers, while nearly all carried rifles erect in their right hands. Sandoval, the Navaho from Cebolleto, was riding back and forth in front of this group, pointing out the error of their ways and warning them of the consequences they might incur when suddenly someone espied a Navaho on a horse that had belonged to a Mexican trooper and had been missing for a couple of days. Word was sent to Colonel Washington, who immediately demanded its return. The Navaho youth riding the horse declared it was his own and immediately disappeared down a side gully. Then the Colonel ordered the Navahos to hand over one of their best horses to replace the one that had been stolen, but as the troopers came toward them, the Navahos became frightened and rode pell-mell

39

down the slope in hasty retreat. The guards were ordered to fire a round of shots after them, and, as there were more than one hundred riflemen in the guard unit, the result was disastrous for the Navahos. They had halted at a little distance to collect their dead and wounded when the cannon sent its missiles among them, thus catching them off guard.

Narbona had been one of the last to retreat and, being in direct line of fire, was mortally wounded. Sixteen or seventeen Navahos were killed outright, and several others died later of the wounds they had received.[4] Narbona lived to reach his hogan and to say farewell to his family. He knew he was about to die, and his last words were, "I am old and it is time for me to go, so do not be sorrowful at my passing, but grieve for the women and children whose men will not return." No other leader has been so long remembered.

[4] In the summer of 1917 I chanced to be riding the Valley Trail near the Two Grey Hills when I saw Mr. Emir James digging in a pit that he thought was a prehistoric burial. As I came nearer I saw a row of skulls grinning at me from the opposite edge, and I asked how many he had found.

"There are seventeen whole and some more crushed in the soil," he replied, but it must have been a poverty-stricken village, for there isn't any pottery to be found." At that time, digging prehistoric ruins was the popular outdoor sport of the few white people living in our section, as there were hundreds of small ruins, each with a nearby burial mound. These mounds often repaid the excavator with an interesting number of artifacts such as pottery, jet beads, shell bracelets, and stone implements.

I dismounted, threw my reins over a bush, and walked around the pit to examine the skulls. I picked one up and turned it over.

"I doubt if these are prehistoric!" I stated as I pointed to the back. "See how it is flattened, a cradleboard did that! You have stumbled on a mass burial of Navahoes!"

"You may be right," Mr. James answered. "Anyway there is nothing to be found here."

As I rode away I could hear him reburying the skeletons and filling the grave. Later I was told by Hosteen Bealle that these were the skeletons of the warriors who had been killed by Colonel Washington's soldiers.

Narbona's family prepared his body for burial. He was bathed and sprinkled with sacred corn pollen, then dressed in his finest buckskin garments with silver buttons and belt. Coral and silver beads and silver bracelets were included, and his feathered helmet was placed on his head. One of his long war bows with its quiver of arrows was placed by his side, and his body was wrapped, together with these items, in several layers of blankets, and then enclosed in a large buffalo pelt which was turned with the fur on the inside. The whole roll was then bound with strand after strand of horsehair rope, tied at intervals into the "death knot."

Toward evening, two of his sons saddled and bridled his two favorite horses, the palomino and the gray stallion, tied his body across the saddles, and proceeded slowly to Rock Mesa, where a deep crevice made a natural tomb. Lowering the bundled body into its final resting place, they covered it deeply with grass and small bushes, on top of which they shoveled a thick layer of earth. They then gathered rocks of every size and distributed them so as to completely hide the burial. When this was done, at sunset, they led the horses some distance to the north, as this was the direction his spirit would take on its journey to the "land of spirits." Since they did not wish to remain near the burial because some enemy might locate the spot and open the grave to obtain the wealth of jewelry it contained, they crossed the valley and stopped on a low hill.

Here they killed the horses and then proceeded to chop the saddles and bridles into small bits so that they could be of no possible use to anyone wandering that way. The ax and the shovel they had used were broken and hidden among the stones. As the darkness gathered, they found a sheltered spot where they could view Rock Mesa, found wood for a small fire, and prepared for a long vigil.

Four nights they remained, chanting prayers throughout the hours of darkness and going only short distances for water or wood during the day. They ate no morsel of food during this time and spoke only with signs or shakes of the head. After the fourth night of prayer they believed the Chief's spirit had traveled so far on the Rainbow Trail that their prayers could not reach him, and the next morning they started for home. When they reached the north bank of the Río Tunicha, they built a sweathouse near some rocks that had been recently piled in that spot and spent that day and night in and out of the sweat bath. The next morning they found the clean clothing their wives had left for them under the stones, and burying all the clothing they had worn during the burial, they went home to feast and sleep.

The army continued its march over Washington Pass and down to the mouth of Canyon de Chelly. Here the treaty was signed by twenty-four chieftains. If the governor and his military advisers believed the death of Narbona would cause the members of the tribe to submit to the terms of the treaty, they were greatly mistaken. In fact, the old Chief was very likely the only one who might have held them to its terms. Now that he was gone, tribal affairs were in the hands of hot-headed young men who, angered by the murder of their leader and the destruction of their farms and homes, were bent on revenge. They even followed the army across the mountain capturing some of the pack mules and stampeding a number of horses.

In 1851, Fort Defiance was established at Bonito Canyon

(called Hell's Hollow by the soldiers), well inside Navaho territory, its avowed purpose to subdue the Navahos or exterminate them. These conditions lasted until 1863, when the Navaho nation was taken captive and marched to the Bosque Redondo. And then the words of the Blind Prophet came true. The Navaho people no longer farmed the fertile valleys or grazed their sheep across the wide mesas. The hungry coyote and the black-winged crow no longer feasted on stray lambs or Navaho corn, and only the Wind Spirits talked to the lonely mountains.

PART TWO

Grandma Klah

5. Girlhood

K LAH'S MOTHER was known by various names during different periods of her life. Throughout her childhood she was familiarly called Zonnie Ahtay or Pretty Girl. Another name used by her family was Tsith-lanai or Mockingbird. As she advanced into her teens, she was taller than most Navaho girls, so then acquired the name of Ahson Tsosie or Slim Woman.

In 1914 when my husband and I started the trading post at Pesh-do-clish (Newcomb, New Mexico), she was living with her daughter and family in the cornfields near our post. Her son Klah lived nearby. At that time Ahson Tsosie was nearly seventy, and her family was composed of one son, Klah, one daughter, Ahdesbah, four granddaughters, and numerous great-grandchildren. To these young people she was Shi-choie or My Grandmother. As some of these girls were part of my household at various times, we too referred to her as "Grandmother." And so she was known as Grandma Klah during the last twenty-one years of her life.

Zonnie Ahtay was four years old when her grandfather, Narbona Tso, was killed by the soldiers in the autumn of 1849. His wives had been dead many years, but he was still the all-powerful patriarch of his family, living in his own hogan, attending the tribal council meetings, and directing the policies of his many followers. Two daughters, who had hogans nearby, cared for his personal needs while their husbands and the children took charge of the flocks and fields. One of these daughters was Chay-endesbah, married to a

Hopi man by the name of Ahyahkini. An expert weaver, he wove belts and garters and ceremonial kilts for the Navahos of this region.

These two were the parents of Zonnie Ahtay, an older sister, and two younger brothers. Her other relatives were four aunts and four uncles living in various parts of the territory claimed by the Navaho tribe. Grandma Klah remembers how she and her brothers and sisters played with dolls made of corn husks and with clay easily molded into small dishes and animal figurines which her mother baked in the earth oven with her own larger pots and ladles. They had no utensils from white people but depended on wicker baskets and water bottles made tight with pitch and on the pottery they molded from native clay.

After Narbona's death, his hogans, flocks, and personal belongings were divided among his children, but the watering places and grazing areas were held as common property. Zonnie Ahtay's parents continued to live at Nee-yai-tsay on the eastern slope of the Chuska Mountains with many of her relatives nearby.

Zonnie Ahtay was too young to remember the years when sheep and goats and cattle were plentiful and when they lived openly and without fear. Their two best horses had been killed near her grandfather's grave, and only a couple of saddle horses were left. They had a small flock of sheep and goats, which were hidden in the brushy mountain swales. There were patches of irrigated farmland on which they raised corn, beans, and plenty of squash and melons. But when the soldiers came, they cut the corn for fodder for their horses and trampled the remainder of the crops into the ground. Several of the Navaho people they knew starved that winter.

Many of her childhood memories are of hasty messengers arriving with warnings of raiding parties of soldiers, Mexicans, or Apaches. Then would come the hurried bundling of blankets, pots, and food supplies into long rolls to be carried on their shoulders as they fled back into the mountains to a hidden cave, where they could find shelter until the raiders were gone.

At this time the governor at Santa Fe and the authorities in Washington were trying to subdue the Navaho tribe to the point where a treaty would be made and kept. They encouraged raids by neighboring tribes of Apaches, Utes, and Puebloans—and they sent bands of soldiers to bring in sheep, cattle, and other food supplies to be used at the forts. Many Navaho men were killed, while the women and children were dragged away to be sold into slavery. It is a wonder that even a remnant of the Navaho tribe remained. But they were tough and desperate and fought back as fiercely as they could, raiding and stealing whenever the opportunity presented itself.

Ahson Tsosie's father died when she was twelve or thirteen, and the last two horses were killed near his grave so that his spirit might have a horse to ride on its last long journey. His wife, Chay-endesbah, became afraid that her two girls might be captured and taken away by the Indians or the soldiers as many others had been. All members of the clan met and decided they must find a safer home at some distant place, and they naturally thought of the wide valleys and high mesas of the Hopi country. Her sisters and their husbands and many children decided to accompany her on a trip to find a new home. Packing their meager possessions into baskets and goatskin bags, they traveled on foot from one watering place to another until they passsed Black Mesa in Arizona and came to a mountain called Ah-whee-yohl-zilth. The whole clan went to this mountain, and that is where they found a place to live near a small river.

On the way they visited with a rich relative who had not been made poor by soldier raids and who had two boys but no girls. He and his wife wished to adopt Slim Woman and promised her mother much goods in exchange. Chay-en-desbah decided that Slim Woman would be safe and well cared for with these relatives, so she gave her to them and went on without her. This uncle, who was called Zilth-yanni Yazzi, was very good to all of them. He was a great hunter and kept them well supplied with deer and antelope meat. His large fields supplied them with melons and squash, part of which were dried and stored for the winter, and also with beans and corn which they ground to make corn-meal. These fields were located near Myah-bi-toh (Coyote Springs), and here they worked all that autumn gathering the crops, digging pits in dry ground where there was no danger of mold, then lining them with cornstalks and leaves to store the squash. The corn and beans were stored in large pottery jars tightly sealed against rodents and hidden in rock crevices. As soon as all was harvested and safely stored, all trace of their labor around the hiding places was obliterated and the family moved again. They dared not stay close to their food supply, as this was near the Ute country where Ute and Apache raids were frequent.

So they moved to Chezzhin (which means Black Rock).

Whenever corn or beans were needed, Zilth-yanni made a trip to his hidden store and brought home a supply. There was much game in this valley, and one time when Slim Woman's foster mother had skinned an antelope, she gave the hide to Slim Woman to make into a dress. When tanned it was a pale yellow and soft as velvet. They cut it into two long pieces to make a straight front and a straight back. These two pieces were laced together at the sides from the armpits to the bottom of the skirt, which was snipped into fine strands to make a fringe which came almost to her ankles. The shoulders were open, but could be tied with leather thongs when she wore it. Her foster mother gave her another piece which she cut into a half-circle and fringed, to make a cape to cover her shoulders and arms. After it was embroidered with porcupine quills, in the manner of the Comanches, Slim Woman thought it the most beautiful dress she had ever seen. This garment was to be worn only on gala occasions such as war dances and religious ceremonials. At this time the Navaho women wore finely woven blanket dresses, generally black or dark blue with bright red and white borders. They tanned deer pelts white for thick leggings and stained the stiffest parts red for shoe leather. Men dressed in suits made of buckskin, decorated with fringe and silver buttons. Some of these suits were red, some were yellow, but the best ones were white.

After leaving Chezzhin they moved to Zilth Lapai (Grey Mountain), near the entrance of a canyon which had a good-sized creek running through it. But this was still nearer the Utes, who were continually stealing their sheep and cattle. Still, it was a pleasant place with water for irrigation and good grassland for the stock. The mountain was covered with cedar and piñon which furnished a supply of nuts and berries and also wood for fires. They stayed here two or three years in spite of continuous Ute raids.

In the spring of 1864, two Navaho men came to bring them word of the march to Bosque Redondo. They described the place as a warm, pleasant land where a river (the Pecos) supplied plenty of water for people, stock, and irrigation. They promised government protection against raiders and government supplies until such a time as the Navahos could raise their own food. To the harassed Navahos this seemed like a picture of the Promised Land. All the Navahos in that section met to discuss the proposition. Zilthyanni had lost many sheep and ponies during the winter and was afraid the time would come when all would be gone. They had not, as yet, planted their store of seed corn, beans, or squash, so it seemed a good time to move to a better location. His brother, Chedilcohie, tried to persuade him to stay and refused to accompany the caravan, saying he intended to move farther south to be away from the Utes.

But Slim Woman's foster mother wanted to go, as she had a sister and brothers who had already started. So they packed their belongings into two canvas-covered wagons, rounded up all their sheep, cattle, and ponies, and started for Tse-hoo-tsosie (Fort Defiance). Nearly all the Navaho families in that section joined the march, and they made a long caravan of horses and wagons, followed by cattle and sheep. The second day on the trail they were attacked by a Ute raiding party and were obliged to scatter in every direction. Before night they came together again, and no one was hurt; but a number of sheep and nearly all the cattle had been driven away.

They traveled all day and all night for three days and nights, and the fourth morning they came to Fort Defiance. Here there were many soldiers riding around to direct the new arrivals to places to camp. Slim Woman had been taught to be afraid of soldiers and tried to hide behind her foster mother. When a soldier came towards them to shake hands with her aunt, she thought he intended to take her away, and she started to cry. He only wanted to show them the commissary, where they were given a large iron kettle and the first matches they had ever seen. Later they were given beef, flour, and salt.

When the camp had been established, they looked around among the assembled Navahos to locate members of their own clan and found Slim Woman's mother and step-father, who were glad to see them and joined their group for the remainder of the journey. Slim Woman's mother had married a Navaho by the name of Dinnae Nez (Tall Man) who came from Huerfano Mesa and was a noted medicine man. The ceremony he practiced was the Female Mountain Chant, sometimes called the Fire Dance, and there were only two others in the Navaho tribe who knew anything about these ceremonial rites. I mention this because in later years Klah was under the tutelage of this man for several years until he had memorized the entire ceremony.

This was the last group of Navahos to be rounded up at Fort Defiance, and after a day spent in counting the number of people, the wagons, the sheep, cattle, and horses, they were lined up and started on the trail to Hweltih. This caravan of twelve hundred people and as many or more ponies, five or six thousand sheep and goats, and three or four hundred cattle, included some of the wealthiest families of the

Navaho tribe, and their wagons were loaded with household goods, food supplies, and seed for starting their new farms. Only the small children and the old or lame rode in the wagons, which were driven by the women. The men, on horseback, herded the sheep and cattle, and the rest of the people walked beside the wagons. Although Zilth-yanni Yazzi had two wagons in the caravan, Slim Woman, her parents, and her foster mother walked most of the way.

6. *Bosque Redondo—The Long Walk*

T HE FIRST STOP was at Shushbi-Toh (Fort Wingate), where there was plenty of water and good grazing. Here their guards were changed, the first group going back to their stations at Fort Defiance. The next stop was at Tohithleen, where again they found good water. The third night they reached the Laguna River, where they rested four days and traded with the Laguna Indians. Two more days brought them to the Río Grande, which was still high from melting snows, but there were several rafts which had been constructed by previous caravans, and these carried them safely across. The crossing was made some distance below the Isleta Pueblo, but all along the river there were houses and farms belonging to Indians, Mexicans, and whites. Here the soldiers gave orders that they were to stay in close formation, for they were marching across Pueblo territory, much against the wishes of the Isleta Indians. Any Navaho who strayed from soldier protection would no doubt be killed. The next day several Navaho families reported that children were missing, but no effort was made to locate them. The next night they camped not far from the east bank of the river, and many went out to gather wood and brush for their cooking fires. As Slim Woman was searching among the rushes, she saw something that looked like a rabbit. Grasping it by its long ears, she found that it was a baby antelope. When the others saw what she had found, they started after her to take it away, but she ran quickly to her uncle Zilth-yanni and gave it to him. Then several white people came and offered to buy it for five or ten dollars, but he refused to sell. That night when they stopped, he tied it in the rushes, and its bleating brought its mother and several other antelope, which were shot with arrows and then eaten. This was repeated for two or three nights, and the fresh antelope meat was very much appreciated by Slim Woman and her family, as they cared little for the rations they were given.

Her family never went hungry since they had their own supply of mutton in addition to the government rations. When her foster mother was issued pork, she took the meat and then gave it away, as she did not think her family would keep well if they ate it. She took the beef, salt, flour, and potatoes that were issued, then dug roots and gathered herbs to season the stew and the mush she made. One stop was at a place of wells, where water gushed out of the ground. It was called Toh-b-dah-des-cloh. The next day at noon they came to Hweltih on the Pecos River. As they entered the reservation, each family was issued a week's rations. Many relatives and friends who had arrived earlier came to greet them, and the confusion was great. Children separated from their parents were not located for days. At first they camped in their wagons and in small canvas shelters supplied by the soldiers. Some adobe houses had been built, but these were occupied by the Mescalero Apaches, who had arrived before the Navahos. They made their camp near the edge of the compound to keep watch over their sheep and goats, for nothing was safe without a guard.

The rations consisted of salted meat, both beef and pork, and when some Navahos saw the salt, they thought it was a poison powder the white people had sprinkled on it. There was whole-wheat flour and baking powder, which they had never seen and were afraid of. Their native way of making bread was with soda made from cedar ashes. They took the coffee beans and boiled them, thinking they were a new kind of pinto bean and would soften into mush. They knew as little about sugar and put a little into all their food, as they did salt. Some put sugar into water and drank sweetened water with their mush. An aunt who had been there for a year taught them the correct way to use these rations and also showed them the wild plants they could eat.

As soon as their camp was established and they located their supply of wood and water, they looked for fields in which to plant their farm seeds. It was getting along into May, and the summer was hot and dry. Where they came from in northern Arizona this was the proper season for planting, but here in the south the seeds should have been in the ground a month before. They were given hoes, shovels, and a plow, with which they worked hard digging out roots and preparing a patch of land for planting. When the seeds sprouted and plants appeared above ground, they tried carrying water from the river to keep the plants alive, but in June a hard sandstorm whipped the corn to ribbons and blasted the squash and melons. Only the beans seemed to withstand the wind and the heat. There was very little food to harvest when autumn came, and they were still obliged to depend on the rations issued by the government.

During the summer the river was low and its waters were bitter with alkali. After the cold mountain water to which they had been accustomed, this was very distasteful to the Navahos, and many of the older people became ill. Sickness became prevalent throughout the compound, and many people died. Slim Woman's mother ate some buffalo meat that had been given them, and that night she bloated rapidly and before morning was dead. A messenger came to their camp to tell her foster mother that her uncle, Tloh-hah-dezi, was very sick and needed someone to take care of him—but her foster mother was cutting up the meat for the stew for their evening meal, so she told the messenger, "I will go in the morning." Her uncle was so ill that night that he could not move when some Apache Indians came and took the logs of his hogan. It stormed in the night, and he died before morning of cold and exposure.

It was shortly after her mother's death that her sister, who had come to Hweltih the year before with her aunt, was married to an Apache and the couple built their house near Zilth-yanni's camp. This Apache (Bay-n-la-Chee) spoke some English and worked for government wages. He received his wages from the commissary in the form of food, clothing, and blankets, which he shared with the whole family, making things a little better after that; but they ate most of their sheep that winter.

The next spring they were given seeds to plant a field near the new irrigation ditch, which they had helped build, and they held their planting ceremonies early in April, so by June the corn was knee high. About the end of the month, there were heavy rains which caused the ditches to over-flow and flood the field. Some of the crops were washed away, and other fields were covered with mud two or three feet deep. So again the Indians faced a winter of semi-star-vation. In late autumn all of the Mescalero Apaches left the reservation and fled southward to their homeland in the Sac-ramento Mountains. This place was declared a reservation, and they still live there. Slim Woman's sister's husband did not go with them, but decided to remain with the Navahos. Sometime during the winter a band of Comanches raided their horse corrals, and there was a battle in which two or three Indians on both sides were killed. One of these was Zilth-yanni's older son. They were very discouraged and wished to return to their homeland, but the government agents persuaded them to stay and plant their fields once more. Firewood was becoming scarce, as the locust, cottonwood, and salt cedars along the river were fast disappearing, and grazing areas for the sheep were difficult to find. Young men and men without families were leaving the compound in groups of five to ten each night. In fact, so many men were leaving that the soldiers were given orders to shoot all deserters. This did little to raise the morale of those who remained or create friendship between the two races.

During the summer of 1866, Slim Woman worked for the wife of an army lieutenant, but she left this employment to be married to a Navaho by the name of Hoskay Nol-yae, who was her senior by ten or twelve years and was quite wealthy in sheep and horses. They did not have a regular marriage ceremony, since there was not enough food to serve many guests. However, her stepfather was a medicine man and chanted the prayers of blessings and, after they had performed the "eating mush" rites, gave them a long exhortation on the duties and responsibilities of married life. They had a hogan in the same locality as her foster parents, and they all worked together. In the spring of 1867, planting was done as usual, but during the last days of May, a gray blanket of army worms covered all vegetation, and when they disappeared there was nothing left. Now indeed

59

this seemed like an evil land. It was too late to plant corn, so the fields were plowed and planted with beans.

Not only had the worms eaten the farm crops, but they had also devoured the grass, weeds, and small shrubs that had furnished food for the sheep. By fall many animals had died and others were too weak to travel to new pastures. Zilth-yanni, Hoskay Nol-yae, and a few other sheep owners begged the commandant to be allowed to move their families and their flocks back to the country from which they had come. The fort was short of supplies and it was now evident that the whole project was a tragic failure, so it is possible that the officers in charge were glad to let them go and to provide them with an escort as far as Bear Springs. Slim Woman was now pregnant, so she and her foster mother were given a place to ride in one of Zilth-Yanni's canvas-covered wagons. After they were loaded and everything was tied tightly in place, Zilth-Yanni and his wife took the driver's seat in one wagon, her aunt and Apache uncle in the other. The sheep, ponies, and goats had started on ahead with Hoskay Nol-yae, the two boys, and several other men as herders, while the wagons waited for the military escort. Everything was wrapped in canvas as far as possible, for they knew they must ford the Río Grande. This did not prove difficult, since the water was low this time of year. The soldiers took them safely past the Isleta and Acoma Pueblos and left them at Fort Wingate.

In April of 1868, Barboncito, Manuelito, Kasuss, and three other Navaho delegates went to Washington to ask the President to be allowed to return to their own country, but they received little hope as the plan then was to send them to Indian Territory (Oklahoma). Later General W. T.

Sherman and Colonel Francis Tappan were sent to Fort Sumner to negotiate a treaty with the Navahos. This treaty gave them only a portion of the land they possessed before leaving for the Bosque, but the Indians were so happy to get away from Fort Sumner and return to Navaho country they were willing to sign almost any agreement. President Andrew Johnson signed the final treaty on June 1, 1868, and in a couple of weeks the Navahos were on their way home.

They were wild with excitement. The men and boys went long distances to raid ranches and pastures for horses and mules, some to ride and others to pull their wagons. A few even rode burros. This time it was not a continuous caravan, as different groups had started whenever they were ready, but each party was accompanied by a group of mounted soldiers to keep them from pillaging the ranches and Indian villages along the way. They were turned over to another group of soldiers at Fort Wingate, and the government counted them, took all their names, and gave them ration cards. Here they joined Zilth-Yanni and his clan, who were camped among the piñon and cedars on the mountainside near the Springs. The general in charge of the fort had instructed them to wait for a shipment of sheep that were to be divided among them.

Slim Woman and her foster parents had arrived at this place in October, but it was a month before her husband and the other men came with the sheep. In December of 1867, Slim Woman gave birth to a baby boy, and this baby grew up to be Hosteen Klah.

Since no sheep or farm implements came to this fort during the winter months to be given to the waiting Indians, they started moving west, to the valleys and mountainsides around Fort Defiance. Here they waited until the summer of 1869 for the promised supplies. When these commodities were finally distributed, each family received one iron Dutch oven, one iron skillet, one water bag, one hoe, one ax, one shovel, twenty yards of trade cloth—red, blue, and tan— and surplus army clothing for the men. Nearly all of the Navaho men were supplied with boots, trousers, wool shirts, caps, and heavy topcoats. There were no clothes for the women, but many army blankets were issued and these made warm shawls.

While they were living here, Slim Woman gave birth to another baby, and this one, much to their joy, was a girl. In the spring, when the mountain snows started to melt, Slim Woman, her husband, her brother, and an aunt and uncle, journeyed over Washington Pass and down the eastern slope of the Chuska Mountains to find Nee-yai-tsay, the home first established by her grandfather, Chief Narbona, from which her mother had fled so many years ago.

HOSTEEN KLAH—medicine man, sand painter, and weaver

GRAY HAIR
who escaped from the Utes after six years of captivity

7. Home and Family

THEY HAD PARTED with Zilth-yanni Yazzi, her foster mother, and their family group at Fort Defiance. These relatives were continuing their journey into Arizona to locate at their old homesites near Chezzhin and to find Zilth-yanni's brother, Cheedilcohie, who had not gone to Hweltih and who now owned many sheep and ponies. Slim Woman was sad to see them leave without her, but she now had a family and must go to the land that was hers by inheritance. When they arrived at the meadow of Nee-yai-tsay, they found nothing left of the hogans, brush shelters, or corrals her parents had built, although outlines of the fields and dikes could still be seen. They did not remain here because there were too many ghosts connected with this place, but continued on to a pleasant swale a few miles away where a sheep corral had been located. They named this place Debeh-b-ghun, and here they built three hogans and a larger sheep corral.

Since the snow on the higher mountain slopes was melting rapidly and they needed farm seeds before this irrigation water was all gone, the aunt, who was the daughter of Narbona's Zuñi wife, went to the Zuñi Pueblo, and her brother, whose father was a Hopi, went to the Hopi Pueblo, both taking part of the trade goods they had been given at Fort Defiance to trade for seeds.

Hoskay Nol-yea had several horses and a flock of sheep, but he did not possess a wagon, so they all traveled on horseback. While waiting for the seeds, Hoskay and his helpers built corrals and dikes, dug irrigation ditches, and flooded his fields. As soon as this water sank into the ground and the seeds had been blessed, he would start the spring planting. It was the Navaho custom to plant the seeds in fairly deep holes which would not soon dry out. The man of the family walked ahead and made the holes with the "planting stick," his wife followed close behind with a blanket full of seeds and dropped a handful into each hole, then brushed earth over them with her foot. The yield was thought to be greater when the seeds were planted by a woman.

The spring was dry and cold, followed by a very hot summer. The corn and beans did not do well, and in the autumn the harvest was scarcely enough to last them through the winter. After another year of hard work and partial crop failure, they were quite discouraged.

The next spring a baby boy was born to Slim Woman. He was fat and healthy and lived to be a year old—then suddenly died. In the morning the baby was all right when she nursed it and then tied it to the cradle-board, but at noon when her aunt wondered why it was so still and went to pick it up, it had stopped breathing. Its face was a mottled gray, its mouth was open, and its tongue had turned black. Slim Woman and her aunt immediately blamed its death on a medicine man who was holding a ceremony not far away. She said, "Those medicine men carry poison darts they can shoot through the air anywhere to kill children and babies." After this there were no more children.

At this time all trade was with trading posts located at Fort Wingate and Fort Defiance under military protection, or with the Jemez and Isleta Indians who traded with the settlers along the Río Grande. They traded silver dollars and turquoise to the Navahos for sheep and goats. Gallup, Flag-staff, and other towns along the Santa Fe Trail had not yet come into being. There were no missions or missionaries nearer than Isleta, but there were some Mormon colonies to the south and west of the Reservation. Several Mormon men married Navaho women and came to live among the Navahos. Some of these were Bi-tsee-lachee (Red Hair), Whuan-ni, Hosteen Zilgathe, Hosteeyi, and Peshlaikai, who was a Mexican silversmith and used silver dollars to make jewelry. All of these seem to have built their homes some-where in the Tunicha Mountains, and their descendants, bearing the same names, are still located there.

After the death of her baby, Slim Woman and Hoskay Nol-yae did not wish to remain at Nee-yai-tsay, so Hoskay located a farm in the Tunicha Valley a few miles below the mesa where Slim Woman's grandfather, Narbona, had been shot by the soldiers. They did not build a permanent house there, but dug an irrigation ditch, enclosed a few acres with dikes, and cleared the ground of brush and roots. After the fields had been flooded and planted, they went back into the Tunicha Mountains behind Toadlena and built three hogans at a place called Des-cheen-di-kana, which means "piñon forest." One house was for Slim Woman's aunt and uncle, another for themselves, and the third for her brother who was now married.

A mountain rill ran down a nearby canyon, and up in the cliffs at the head of this same canyon were hidden caves which furnished hiding places when Ute raiders came across the San Juan River. The United States soldiers had been taken from both Fort Defiance and Fort Wingate and trans-ported east to fight the Civil War, so the Navaho families, with no means of defense, were completely at the mercy of roving bands of Utes and Apaches. These raiders sold the captured women and children to the Mexicans for slaves and in return received horses and cattle. There was not much danger of raids during the winter or spring months, so the Hoskay Nol-yae family built snug adobe hogans near Black Dike Springs in the lower Tunicha Valley and brought their livestock here where the tall grass would furnish grazing for the winter months. These hogans were covered with native adobe and so resembled the earth and nearby rocks that they blended into the landscape and were practically invisible at any distance.

In the spring they built brush shelters near their fields and lived there until the planting was finished. Then these shelters were destroyed, all evidence of their residence in that place was obliterated, and the family, with flocks and household goods, moved to their summer home at Descheen-di-kana. During the summer many trips were made to the cornfields to hoe the weeds and to make the best use of irrigation water when the summer rains filled the arroyos and the ditches. At this time Tunicha Creek (later to be known as Captain Tom's Wash) carried more water than it does now. Snow melting on the mountains filled it with water from March, when irrigating began, until late in May. June was a dry month and the water in the creek was reduced to a trickle, but July was the month of summer storms that often turned the creek into a raging torrent which overflowed its banks and turned the lower meadows into lakes. Through August and the autumn months there were rains on the mountains which furnished the creek with a constant stream. During harvest season, Slim Woman and her family again built shelters near the fields where they could live while harvesting their crops. Again pits were dug some distance from the fields, corn, beans, and squash were stored, and the place was carefully camouflaged.

She did not mention guards stationed to the north to warn them of approaching raiders, but there may have been. She did tell of one time when they were sent word that a party of Utes were traveling toward them and there was not time to reach a hiding place in the mountains. Her husband said it would be better to travel towards the Utes than away from them. So they and all the other Navahos working there put their shoes on backward and traveled all night toward the north. They walked in single file and stepped in each other's tracks as nearly as possible. Before daylight arrived they were all hidden behind the bank of the big bend in the Tsay-nas-tee Canyon. The Utes rode south to the Tunicha Valley, burned all the hogans, killed as many sheep as they could find, and had a feast of corn, melons, and mutton. When they discovered the trail of the fugitives, it was too late to catch them, for the Navahos had fled to the mountains and were safely hidden.

Years passed and changes came to the Navaho Reservation. Schools were built and agencies established, missionaries erected missions at various places, and trading posts were built, first near the schools and then in a network that spread over the entire Reservation. Navaho hand-woven blankets were much in demand and became one of their main sources of income. Slim Woman, who now was known as Ahson Tso or Large Woman, had learned from her Hopi father how to spin the wool into a fine, hard-twisted yarn and to weave it into a brightly patterned rug. These finer rugs brought the highest prices. After her aunt died, Ahson Tso taught her son, Klah, and her daughter, Ahdesbah, to weave in the same manner, but she never trusted them to spin the yarn. Her reputation as an expert spinner lasted as long as she could see, and most of the yarn Hosteen Klah used in his sand-painting rugs was spun by his mother.

Peace and prosperity had come to Ahson Tso and her family. Hoskay Nol-yae bought a wagon, a plow, and a number of cattle. The flock of sheep owned by the family group numbered more than one thousand besides one hundred or more goats. Each spring at lambing time Hoskay gave each of his children a number of lambs with which to start their own flocks. During the many years they were together, the Hoskay Nol-yae family were among the most important and respected people on the Reservation.

In 1914, when I first met Grandma Klah, she was sixty-nine years old, but as strong and active as many women of forty. She lived in a hogan near that of her daughter, Ahdesbah, who had been married twice and had four daughters. Why none of these daughters had ever been sent to government boarding schools, I do not know.

Grandma Klah still owned two or three hundred sheep and was still an industrious weaver. Many Navaho families brought their wool to her to be spun into weaving yarn, and in return she was given some of the wool as payment for her labor. She herded not only her own sheep, but also the entire flock belonging to her family. I can still see her trudging behind the noisy flock, slightly bent and a bit lame, swinging a long stick on the end of which was tied a tin can filled with pebbles, which she used as both rattle and cane.

She not only helped with the herding but also with the

shearing. When the wool clip was brought to the post to be weighed and sold, she came with the others and counted out her share of the silver dollars, fleece by fleece. After placing part of the silver in a moneybag which she concealed under her full skirt, she piled the remaining dollars into equal piles, one for each member of her family. Then she sat comfortably on the floor and watched while they proceeded to spend her money.

Early in the 1920's, her daughter, Ahdesbah, was thrown from her horse and suffered a dislocated shoulder and a broken collar bone. Her shoulder may have been fractured, for not long afterward a wen as large as a goose egg appeared on her back not far from the shoulder joint. Two or three healing ceremonies were held for her, but none removed the wen or gave her back the use of that arm. Finally, an old medicine man who sang the Knife Chant was called, and after a five-day ceremony, the wen was gone and she slowly regained partial use of her arm. Just how the old chanter removed the wen I was never able to find out, but Navaho medicine men do perform minor surgery when the occasion requires. Grandma Klah took care of her daughter through this illness, assuming all of the extra work along with her own tasks, until Ahdesbah was fully recovered. But the injured arm was always stiff, and Ahdesbah could not card or spin the wool, although she could still dye the yarn and help with the weaving.[1]

---

[1] The heart, liver, and entrails of a slaughtered animal are never cooked and used for food. These are called "coyote food" and are generally tossed into a ditch out of sight and left for the dogs and coyotes to quarrel over. Sometimes a midwife takes the heart of a goat or a beef and boils it over a slow fire. Then she cuts it into strips which are allowed to dry, after which they are ground into powder. This she carries with

As the years passed, Grandma Klah gave more and more of her sheep to her grandchildren and had it understood that when she was gone, Evelyn should have all that remained. Evelyn was a baby when her mother died of flu and Grandma Klah had taken her to raise, so she was her favorite granddaughter. There never seemed to be any jealousy about this among the others, the consensus of opinion seeming to be that "the sheep belong to Grandma and she has a right to give them to whomever she pleases."

One day Grandma Klah came to our post with a rug to sell. When a purchase price had been agreed upon, she carefully counted her silver dollars and then paid for a double string of coral beads she had placed in pawn several months before. With the remainder of the money she first bought shoes for Evelyn and then bought dark blue velveteen for a blouse, many yards of black sateen for a full skirt, and a beautiful, long-fringed Pendleton shawl. She bargained for each article separately, counting her money over and over after each purchase. When I asked her granddaughter if Grandma was planning to have a ceremony held for her, she answered, "No, she will pay us for making these clothes for her, and then she will put them away for burial garments so she can enter the next world well dressed."

Although there was always plenty of food, Grandma ate sparingly, for the many years of semistarvation never were forgotten. She was never happy unless she was busy at some useful task. Herding sheep, caring for babies, hoeing corn, carding, weaving, or spinning, she was never idle. When cataracts at last nearly covered her eyes, she could not fol-

---

her on her "cases" to make broth to strengthen the new mother. Sheep or lamb hearts are not used.

low the sheep or hoe the corn. She wove her last blanket at the age of eighty-two when she was partially blind. Her granddaughters strung the warp on the loom and gave her black and white wool to use, as she could still distinguish between light and dark. It was not well woven and the pattern was uneven, but I kept it as one of my prized possessions until it was burned in the fire that destroyed our trading post.

One of her granddaughters had died during the flu epidemic of 1919, but Grandma taught the remaining three to spin fine yarn and weave compact blankets that brought high prices and were always in demand. The two older girls (Mrs. Sam and Mrs. Jim) later wove sand-painting blankets under the direction of their uncle, Hosteen Klah, and these are preserved in museums in many parts of the United States. The younger girl, Daisy Tahgahl-chee, became noted as the best weaver on the Navaho Reservation.

On September 14, 1935, this article appeared in the *Southwest Tourist News,* a paper published in Gallup, New Mexico, by M. L. Woodard:

> Grandma Klah—On the 17th of August, Grandma Klah, who might rightfully have claimed the title of "Navajo Princess," closed her eyes in the last long sleep. If she had lived until August 31st she would have been ninety years old. Crippled, blind, and deaf, she was mentally alert until the day of her death, and although quite helpless, was well cared for, loved, and respected by her grand-children and great-grand-children. The family who survive her passing comprise of one son, Hosteen Klah, a noted Medicine-man; one daughter, three grand-daughters, several great-grand-children, and one great-great-grandson. Grandma Klah was born the summer the United States made the Nuby treaty with

the Navajo Indians. She was four years old when her grand-father, the noted Chief Narbona, whose Navajo name was Nahtohnie Tso, was shot and killed by the soldiers of the Simpson expedition.

Grandma Klah was a tall maiden called Slim Girl and later known as Ahson Tso, meaning, Large Woman. During the last years of her life her thoughts traveled back to her girlhood—to the scenes and events of a past generation. She told of traveling four days, with her mother and father to Ft. Wingate, in order to see if the people stationed there were really WHITE. She told of the Utes and the soldiers who raided her father's flocks and fields forcing the family to live in a hidden canyon in Rock Mesa. She told of the journey to the Bosque Redondo and her experiences while there, and then the return to a ravaged homeland. Always she completed these tales with a weary sigh and the words, "It was a long walk." And so, with the passing of Grandma Klah, one of the most dramatic eras of Navajo history came to a close.

PART THREE

Hosteen Klah

8. Boyhood at Nee-yai-tsay

THE SUMMER OF 1867, with drought and a devastating plague of army worms, brought complete despair to the Navaho farmers at the Bosque Redondo. By August they knew there would be no corn to harvest and no fodder for their sheep and horses. Many of their older people had died, among them a number of their most powerful medicine men, and they began to feel that their gods had deserted them. Everyone began to plan some way to leave this unlucky country.

Long before word came from Washington granting them a reservation in their home territory, Zilth-yanni and his family had been packing their belongings, mending the two wagons, buying new canvas, and selling the weakest of their sheep and goats since only the strong would be able to make the trip back to Fort Defiance. Even before the treaty with the government was signed, they were on the move. Ahson Tsosie and her husband, Hoskay Nol-yae, had sheep and goats but no wagon, so their household goods were loaded with those of her aunt. Ahson Tsosie and her foster mother drove one four-horse team pulling a canvas-covered wagon, and her aunt and uncle drove the other. Most of the men rode horseback to herd the sheep.

Many other Navaho families started with them, some with horses and wagons or burros and mules, but many on foot. They were given a military escort as far as Bear Springs (Fort Wingate), which was then in Navaho territory. Here they were turned over to the Indian agent and were counted in order to receive government rations. Among the trees behind the agency they made a temporary camp between their wagons where they waited four or five weeks for their men to arrive with the sheep. Then they all moved back to a sheltered cove on Bear Mountain and built semipermanent living quarters in which to stay through the winter.

The commissioner of Indian affairs in Washington had sent word that all Navaho families should remain near Fort Wingate until the government could buy a large flock of sheep to be distributed among them. Only a few of the most prosperous Navahos still owned flocks of sheep and goats, and there were no cattle. The agent at the fort issued rations of flour, salt, sugar, coffee, and sometimes fresh beef, but there was never any certainty when these supplies would arrive, and when they did, there was seldom enough for all, so the poorer Navahos were often hungry. October frosts had opened the piñon burs and the pine cones, so the Navahos spent the crisp autumn days gathering nuts to store for the winter. Sunflower seeds, wild millet, cactus fruit, and rose hips were also gathered.

In the latter part of October, Ahson Tsosie gave birth to a baby boy who was destined to become the most noted medicine man on the Navaho Reservation. In preparation for the birth a small hut had been built at some distance from the cluster of hogans that housed the several families, and to it Ahson Tsosie went with her aunt, who was a midwife. A bitter tea made from the root of Azzay-nah-ol-todie (white daisy) was brewed for her to drink since it would cause a quick delivery. Afterwards she was given several cups of spruce tea.

Her uncle, who was a Hail Chant medicine man, had

accompanied the women and chanted prayers over Ahson Tsosie and the new baby. As soon as the child was breathing evenly, he was given a sponge bath with a herb infusion and then was thoroughly greased with melted goat tallow. No clothing had been prepared before his birth, for that would have brought bad luck, but the aunt had a square of soft buckskin which she used for a blanket. The baby was placed on the pallet beside his mother with the top of his head toward the central fire. If it had been a warm, sunny day, the top of his head would have been put in the sunshine, since heat was thought to be necessary for a baby to grow tall and strong like the corn or the sunflower.

Ahson Tsosie and the baby stayed in the shelter four days and four nights, being cared for by the aunt and uncle, before Hoskay Nol-yae was notified that he had a son and the birth was announced to the rest of the family. If during this time the baby had died, it would have been quietly buried and never have been counted as being alive. On the fifth day the father came to see it, bringing soft away-tsal cotton for its bed and two well-tanned kid pelts for the covers. As the weeks passed, the baby was occasionally fed a little mare's milk to build strong bones and teeth; to insure a strong heart, it was given broth from stewed goat's hearts.

No name was given at this time, only "Away Eskay," meaning "Baby Boy," which is the name of all Navaho boy babies before they exhibit some characteristic or some unusual mark is discovered on their bodies to suggest a name. The latter is only a nickname, however, for, after their naming rites, they are given a ceremonial name, which is considered their personal property and seldom known to anyone outside their immediate family. It was four or five years after his birth that this boy was given the nickname that remained with him throughout his life. It was noticed that he used his left hand more readily than his right, so he was called "Klah," which means "left-handed."

For four or five months, this group lived in the mountains near Bear Springs waiting for the government sheep. But when there was no word of their coming, the group decided to move to Fort Defiance, where they might find better pasture. Again all of their possessions were packed and loaded on the wagons, and they were on the move, with the sheep trailing behind. It was only sixty miles to the fort, but it was a mountainous trail and they traveled slowly, advancing not more than ten miles each day, stopping wherever the grass was plentiful to allow the sheep to graze. They found many other family groups living in temporary camps all around the fort. There was no room for them, so they turned north and found a valley with a small lake near the foot of the Tohatchi Mountains, and here they stayed almost a year.

It was the winter of 1868–69 when the government sheep finally arrived, and each Navaho man, woman, and child was given two. So Klah, at the age of one year, became a sheepowner. This did not mean as much to him then as did the cradleboard his father made for him while they were at this place. Two straight pine boards about five inches longer than the baby were laced together in the center, and a small board was laced at the bottom to form a footboard. Then a thin lath of ash was bent across the top, just above where his head would be, to hold the covers away from his face. Smaller sidepieces were fastened to the bottom boards and holes were bored in them so that

MAD WOMAN
who was kidnaped on the way to the Bosque Redondo

MEDICINE WOMAN AND SON
she made "The Long Walk" to the Bosque Redondo

buckskin thongs could be threaded through them and, when laced back and forth, would hold the baby safely in place. A thick pad of away-tsal cotton and the two kid pelts completed Klah's baby bed, which from that time was his own private property and would never be used by any other child. A strong leather strap was fastened to the top in a loop that would reach across his mother's chest, enabling her to carry the cradle on her back. This gave her the use of her hands while carrying the baby and was a great convenience when riding horseback. The cradle also kept the baby from crawling into the open fire or coming to harm in other ways.

Again, food became a major problem. The government issue of rations was more generous here but was often late in arriving, and the Navaho families could not depend on it. They had brought some corn from the Bosque Redondo and had bought corn and beans from the Puebloans along the way. They parched the corn and ground it with piñon nut meats or with sunflower seeds, which are rich in oil, to make flat cakes that were very good when toasted on hot stones. They used the tart berries of the nahl-tsosie to boil with goat milk to make cheese; this is the same plant whose fleshy root is crushed to make a paste for toothache medicine. Ahson Tsosie's aunt, who had much knowledge of plants and herb medicines, searched the mountainsides for crow onions, wild mustard, pepper grass, beeweed pods, sage, mint, and many other herbs used for healing. With this addition to their rations, they managed to stay strong and well until the arrival of the promised sheep.

When every family had received its quota of government goods and sheep, they separated, each clan journey-

79

ing to its own homeland, as did the Jews returning to Jerusalem in the time of the Babylonian captivity. Zilth-yanni and all of his family continued west to the Hopi country. Ahson Tsosie, Hoskay Nol-yae, the baby, both of her brothers, an older sister, two aunts, and one uncle crossed the Cottonwood Pass and came to their old home at Nee-yai-tsay. Their first hogans were built at a place they called Debeh-b-ghun, as it was near an old sheep corral and was not far from Debeh-b-toh (Sheep Springs), with grass-filled valleys on two sides.

Government rations were now a thing of the past, and the winter had exhausted their corn and nuts. But it seems that there was always something provided by Providence. During the years of their absence, the few horses that had been abandoned in the canyons had multiplied until wild herds were to be found ranging through every valley and watering at every spring. Hoskay Nol-yae and other Navaho men soon built high corrals to capture a few at a time, as they wished to tame the colts for their own use and kill the wildest ones for meat. Some of these horses they traded to the Zuñi and the Laguna Indians for corn and beans and to the Mexican ranchers for goats.

Thus their small flocks of sheep were held intact, and in the spring there was a good crop of lambs which more than doubled their number and gave the Navahos wool for weaving and mutton for feast days.

About this time, the Indian Office in Washington decided to take a census of all Navahos living on the Reservation; to do so, they offered one sheep to every Navaho who would come to Fort Defiance to be counted. This census was not a complete success, for many families living at a distance refused to come. Hoskay Nol-yae and all of his clan went and received more than fifteen sheep. Their flock was now beginning to be of such size that when the autumn harvest had been gathered and stored, they need not look forward to another winter of semi-starvation.

Klah remembered living at Des-cheen-di-kana in the cedars, as most of his boyhood was spent there and at the home near the Black Dike. He remembered the wide corn-fields which were irrigated twice each year, once before planting time when the arroyos overflowed with water from the mountains' melting snows, and once in midsummer when seasonal rains filled the irrigation ditches. He told of helping with the harvest and storing the corn and beans in pits where they would be safe from wandering bands of Ute or Apaches, and he told of shearing time, which was an outstanding event in the life of any small Navaho boy.

When the time came to shear the sheep in April or May, a secondary corral was built near the home corral and a number of expert shearers were engaged to do the shearing. A flock of sheep would be driven into the new corral and each shearer would take one out and clip its coat. The wool did not come off in bits or bunches, but in one entire fleece, which was tossed to a Navaho packer. Large wool sacks were attached to a frame and the packer stood inside each in turn to stomp the wool down tight as it came to him, fleece by fleece. The shearers vied with each other in regard to the time required to shear a sheep and the smoothness of the fleece. To clip through a sheep's hide so that there was even one drop of blood was a black mark on the shearer's record. The shorn sheep was handed over to another helper who, with black tar, made the owner's brand between its ears and shoved it into the larger corral.

It was the custom for all families in that area to use the same corrals and employ the same shearers, whose pay was a share of the wool. Both men and women helped with the shearing, which required strong arms and backs. The older women baked quantities of oven bread, pan-fried *tortillas*, and blue-corn tamales wrapped in corn husks, then baked under hot ashes. A goat, generally an old one, was killed and roasted in a pit filled with hot coals. It was stuffed with corn leaves, mint, sage, pepper grass, and wild mustard, then well salted before being placed in the pit, where it was thickly covered with corn leaves and a layer of earth. A steady fire was kept burning on top for half the day. There were big black pots of coffee and kettles of beans cooked with peppers. Women worked, ate, and gossiped; men toiled, sweated, and feasted; children ran and played, cried and laughed, and ate all their mothers handed them. Shearing time and planting time were the two spring festival seasons when all worked together.

Perhaps half of the white wool and all of the brown wool was kept at home for weaving. There was a growing demand at the trading posts for Navaho blankets, and at that time the Navahos still wore dresses and blankets of their own weaving. The wool to be sold was taken to traders at Fort Defiance or to Mormon traders at Joseph City, where it was exchanged for coffee, sugar, canned fruit, velveteen, calico, farm implements, and other trade goods. This was the last trading the family (the whole family went on these trips) would do until they sold their surplus sheep in the fall. It was on one of these trading trips that Klah saw his first white people, and he wondered if they were painted and if the paint would rub off. There was a man with a large head of bushy hair and hair all over his face. This astonished Klah for none of his family had hair on their faces. There was a woman with yellow hair and blue eyes; he wondered if she could really see with such queer eyes, and then he remembered that coyotes had yellow eyes and could see in the dark. He decided to like the woman because she gave him two sticks of peppermint candy, one for himself and one for his sister, who was hiding behind their mother's full skirts.

His mother's aunt and uncle were with them on this trip, and the aunt bought him a pair of boots—the first store footwear he had ever possessed. He decided that they were much too wonderful to wear and he would keep them to look at. Since he was very observant and remembered everything he saw, this trip gave him much to think about, and he resolved to go as often as he could to see these white strangers who had so many amazing things in their big stone houses.

That fall his mother and father took him to the Zuñi Pueblo to trade a blanket his mother had woven for cakes of salt for the sheep and cattle and for reed baskets filled with salt for their own use. He saw stone houses again and his first orchards. Peaches were ripe, and his mother bought a basket of them to take home. Klah bit into one and decided it tasted very good, but he did not like the Zuñi people because they had such long bangs hanging over their faces he could hardly see their eyes. He did not care to go there again, although his mother and father went every year to obtain salt and fruit.

Klah was a small boy when a government boarding school was built at Grand Junction, Colorado. A school organizer came to Tunicha Valley and asked his parents to send their children to school when the agency wagons came for them. The families with several children of school age did send part of them to this school, not so much to have their children educated as to keep them safely away from the Utes. Dudley Dijolei was one who went and received a good education, but he did not see his parents for six years. He returned to marry and live in Tunicha Valley, where he became a well-known medicine man who sang the Shooting Chant. Ahson Tsosie did not send either Klah or Ahdesbah to this school, as she had only the two and needed their help at home. Navaho children begin very early in life to help with such tasks as gathering sticks for the hogan fires, shelling the corn, and keeping the water bucket filled.

Ahson Tsosie's aunt and uncle were growing old, but the aunt still did the spinning and dyeing of the yarn and most of the cooking and housework. The uncle helped Ahson Tsosie with the sheep when Hoskay Nol-yae was away trailing horses, for there were now several hundred sheep and their care was too much for one person.

The uncle was a medicine man who sang the Hail Chant, and his services were in frequent demand for sick people in different parts of the area. He liked to take Klah with him to these ceremonies since Klah could help him with many small tasks. It was on these occasions that the young boy learned this chant, and he was probably one of the youngest Navaho boys to know a full ceremony. He could direct the sand paintings, sing the correct prayer chants, and conduct the rites by the time he was ten years old, and he may have known more about the herbs and pollens to be used than his uncle. He had often accompanied his aunt, who may have been part Hopi, on her frequent trips to the mountains and creeks to gather herbs, berries, roots, and bark to use for various purposes. She was a learned herbalist and could give a name to almost everything that grew within her range of travel. She had ways of telling which plants were poisonous, which were food for animals or birds, and which could be used by humans for food or medicine. She taught Klah that everything growing had some useful purpose, that even the nightshade, the poison sumac, and the yellow dock could be used for making dye for their blankets. He never forgot her teachings.

When Klah was eight years old, and large for his age, he was given the task of caring for the big herd of horses they now owned. Horses had added much to the Navaho economy in his great-grandfather's time, and now they were helping his family gain a comfortable prosperity. Hoskay Nol-yae occasionally took Klah with him on his trips to round up wild mares to be sold to the Mexicans or to the Navahos on the other side of the mountains. Klah's own pony was a sure-footed bay mare that had never run with the wild ones and would come to him when he held out an ear of corn.

The horses they were able to catch were always branded by clipping a distinctive notch (or perhaps two) in one ear; this was their own brand, and wherever the horse roamed for pasture or water, they could claim ownership when they wanted it. Some of their sheep and most of their goats were marked in the same manner. One week in fall was given over to branding, castrating, and taming wild horses. It was not a festival, as there were no women concerned with it and no great quantities of food were prepared, but it was a very exciting time for the young men and boys.

The horses were fat and frisky from a summer of mountain grazing and had entirely forgotten that humans were their masters. It was quite a problem to haze them into the corral, and more of a problem to get a rope around any neck. What a thunder of hoofs as they circled inside the corral, almost invisible in the cloud of dust that was raised, and what a wild stampede when the ones desired had been roped and the others turned loose! It was a stouthearted lad who would volunteer to ride one of the "wild" ones.

After the first rope was secure around the horse's neck, it was not so difficult to get another on a hind leg and pull the animal to the corral fence where the rider was perched, ready to leap on its back, sans saddle, sans bridle, spurs, or whip. Then the rider's friends hung on to the lariats with all their strength while he clung to the horse's mane, until the animal, half-choked and white with lather, would pause to gasp for breath. Then the rider would leap to the ground, climb the corral fence, and be greeted with cheers and admiration. He had ridden his horse to a stand-still! This was really more a stunt of bravado than an actual attempt to tame the horse, but many a young Navaho gained his reputation as a horse wrangler in this manner.

It was a sunny September morning when a rider came galloping from the north to say that a party of raiding Utes had crossed the San Juan River and reached the Sulphur Springs. All of the Tunicha Valley farmers were living around their cornfields, and there were only a few horses anywhere near. The news spread, and everyone gathered in a group to make plans. The old folks and the mothers with babies would take sacks of food and start at once for the first Gray Butte, and after following its one path to the top, they could block the passage with stones so that no one could reach them. Herders would mount the few horses and drive the sheep along behind the old folks and women to obliterate their trail. When the junipers had been reached, the boys would scatter the sheep far and wide among the bushes and arroyos and immediately ride to the hiding places in the mountains. Klah was one of the boys who herded the sheep. The main group of Navahos would pack everything they could carry on their backs and walk toward the Ute war party, who would probably camp that night at Toh-tse-toh Springs. They took time to bury the corn that had been harvested and some of their farm implements, then they started walking single file, keeping to the low ground and valleys. Before morning, they had reached the deep Tsay-nas-tee Canyon. Here they rested while scouts reported the progress of the Utes, who were again headed south, never dreaming that the Navahos were just a couple of miles west of them. As soon as the Utes had ridden far enough away for them to be safe, the Navahos started for the mountains where their winter homes were located and where there were many small caves.

When the Utes reached the cornfields, they were angry to find them deserted. No slaves to be captured, no horses to take home, and no Navahos to engage in battle! They found a few sheep, which they killed and roasted, and then had a feast of melons, roasting ears, and mutton. They burned the temporary brush houses and rode their horses over the fields, trampling the crops into the ground. Then they turned and rode back to their own reservation at Ute Mountain. This may have been the last time a large party of Ute raiders ever came as far south as the Tunicha Valley.

9. *Life with an Apache Uncle*

THE RESULTS of the Ute raid were not so disastrous to the Navahos in Tunicha Valley as in former years, for now they did not do all their planting in one place. There were glades and meadows on the mountainside that could be irrigated to raise melons, potatoes, and squash, as well as corn. The majority of the sheep were rounded up and brought to the corrals, but—most fortunate of all—no one had been killed or hurt, and no women or children had been taken captive. A small percentage of the corn and beans had not been damaged, so a few families went back to the cornfields, built new shelters, and stayed to harvest this remnant.

Ahson Tsosie and Hoskay Nol-yae decided that this country was too near the Utes and too dangerous for a boy who was now old enough to be riding near and far by himself. Klah's mother had an aunt who had married a Mescalero Apache while at the Bosque Redondo and who now lived on the western slope of the Lukachukai Mountains. Packing their horses for a three-day trip, the family of four rode over the Pass and along the western slopes to the home of this aunt and her husband. They stayed several days talking things over, as Navahos never approach a problem directly, but mention everything else first and carefully pave the way to stating the main object of the visit.

Finally an agreement was reached by which Klah would remain a year or two with these relatives with the status of "grandson," and his parents would pay for his board with goats, sheep, and a couple of horses. The aunt and uncle would bring him home for visits two or three times each year and collect the payments. Klah was intrigued with new people and new places. He had his pony and his bow and arrows, and he knew he would enjoy exploring this side of the mountains.

They did not leave Ahdesbah here as she, being a girl and always near her mother, was in little danger of being kidnaped. Besides, her mother needed her help with the sheep and the weaving.

Klah soon discovered that this side of the mountains was quite different from the side where he had been living. Only the crests were rocky, then the whole range sloped gradually but majestically down to glades and mesas where the land was almost level. These soon sheared off, and another slope began. It was tree country, but not in the manner he knew, where the cedar, spruce, and piñon, crowding each other in tangled clusters, spread their branches close to the ground to hold the moisture and protect their roots. Here the great Norway pines stood far apart with mottled trunks like temple pillars, standing bare as far as Klah could reach, then branching thickly the remainder of their height. Even the piñon and the cedars had no low branches but stood quite tall with foliage at the upper part. There was little brush because of the grazing of generations of goats, but the slopes were covered with grasses, lupine, horsemint, Indian paintbrush, and more shrubs and plants than he could name. He wished his great-aunt could be here to collect and tell him all about them.

Every small canyon carried a creek, winding its way

through tangled thickets of willow, pin cherry, witch hazel, sumac, and black haw bushes, to form small lakes and marshy fens in the swales. These never went dry, and around them could be found bulrushes, cane grass, cowslips, trillium, and other plants that grow near water. Klah thought this could well be a herb-gatherer's paradise.

The Navahos on this side of the mountains had no need for two dwelling places. Their clusters of hogans were built among the trees at walking distance from their water supply, and generally some little distance up the slope above the swales where their farms were located. These farms were not extensive, being patches of slanting land that could be irrigated from the creek, but they were usually productive because there had never been a dry season. The flocks were mostly goats, which did not sicken and die in high altitudes. A few sheep were kept for their wool, which could be carded with the mohair of the goats and spun into a silky yarn that made beautiful blankets. There were no wild herds of horses, but each family owned several saddle ponies and a team for the wagon.

These animals grazed on the herbage of nearby slopes, but all were brought to the home corrals at night. Although there were not many coyotes on this side of the mountains, there was danger from an occasional cougar, and bears were numerous. In Navaho country, a bear is seldom killed, but cougars are hunted down with all possible speed. If tracks of this big cat are seen around the corrals or watering places, the best hunters arm themselves and start in pursuit with an experienced tracker in the lead. This family owned no dogs that would follow the trail of this dangerous animal, but they did not need dogs. Navaho trackers are perhaps the best in the world, and once started on a trail, there would be no pause until the quarry was located. The Navaho man who killed the cougar could claim its hide, which would be tanned and used to make a quiver for his hunting arrows and thongs to tie medicine bundles. The other hunters took sinews, heart, and fangs, while each member of the party had one cougar claw to hang on a string around his neck, indicating that he had killed one cougar. It was a mighty hunter who could wear a whole necklace of cougar claws.

Black and brown bears were numerous among the mountain cliffs, where they wintered in deep caves and wandered the slopes in summer to live on berries, fat tree grubs, acorns, and piñon nuts. The Navahos regarded them with almost as much respect as they gave their human neighbors, killing them only when necessary to save a life or to protect their flocks. Under no conditions would a Navaho eat a bite of bear meat. One young Navaho remarked, "I wouldn't eat bear meat. I might be chewing on the spirit of one of my ancestors." The bear is a totemic animal often mentioned in myth and legend; many chants and sand paintings are given in his honor.

Klah saw his first bear on a ride up a thickly wooded ravine. Two young brown bears were clawing at a rotten log lying across the ditch to peal the bark and expose the white grubs underneath. His pony scented the animals and would have run away, but he held it still and soon saw the cause of its fright. Since his pony had made quite a clatter, the bears must have known he was there, but they paid no heed to him and kept diligently at the task of finding food. Klah knew several of the "Bear Songs," which he now chanted to secure their good will before riding back the way he had come.

Klah spent much time riding along the mountain slopes and up the canyons. One afternoon as he was exploring one of these canyons, he discovered the mouth of a cave high in the cliffs above him. Leaving his horse tied to a bush, he carefully worked his way up the steep wall of rock until he finally came to a narrow ledge that furnished a trail to the cave. Its mouth was partially blocked with loose stones and tangled brush and rubble from above, so he approached with care to keep from causing another rockslide. He knew there were no snakes at this high altitude and the bears were out of hibernation now, but there might be a mountain lioness with kittens. Noting a wide ledge above the opening, he found another path and clambered up to it. Lying flat on his stomach, he could peer over the edge and view the whole interior of the cave. When his eyes had become accustomed to its dimness, he could see that it was wide and roomy but not very deep, being somewhat the shape of a flattened pottery bowl with no sharp corners. On the floor was a curious assortment of objects which he could hardly name because of the thick coat of dust which blanketed them and dimmed the outlines.

Three large pottery jars were easily identified because of their shape; rolls of what might be buckskin or buffalo pelts lay beside them; the coils of ceremonial baskets appeared dimly; but to the other mounds and bundles he could give no name. The most surprising and awe-inspiring sight of all was the painted figures on the walls. The surface of these walls must have been smoothed by hand to make a canvas for all the immortals in the Yeibichai pantheon. There stood the Talking God, the House God, the Rain Maker, the Fire God, the Humpback Twins, the Warrior and his Brother, the Yeibaka and the Yeibaade, and four Flint People, all marching in solemn procession around the walls, clothed in elaborate ceremonial costumes, the colors of which were as bright and clear as the day they were painted. He was too overcome to do more than clamber down the cliff, mount his pony, and find his way home.

His uncle was as excited about his discovery as Klah had been, and the next morning they both rode up the canyon to the cave. After clearing away some loose stones that had once formed a wall to conceal the mouth of the cave and tossing out the brush, they finally stepped inside. The floor was smooth and sandy, the walls were about twice their own height, and the ceiling arched smoothly above. The pottery and bundles occupied one-third of the floor space near the rear wall, while other objects were scattered about. The painted figures stared at them through slits in their ceremonial masks.

"Do you think this is a cave where the Anat-sazie buried their dead?" Klah asked his uncle, who was studying each object carefully. "Or is it the burial of a Navaho medicine man?"

"It is not of the Old Ones," his uncle answered, "for they did not know of the Yeibichai gods, and I see no signs of a burial anywhere."

Carefully he fanned the dust from the huge jars and found them to be unsealed. Whatever corn, seeds, or water had been stored here had long since disappeared. He touched a bundle that evidently had held either eagle or

CHIEF NARBONA
Klah's great-grandfather

Grandma Klah *(center)*, Ahdesbah, and Klah

turkey feathers, and a cloud of dust came up to choke him; they were now just a bundle of quills. The medicine bundles rolled in buckskin he did not touch, for he knew they would crack into bits if disturbed.

One small flint arrowhead Klah picked out of the dust and showed to his uncle. "I would like to keep this as a good luck piece, if you think it would be right to do so."

His uncle nodded: "It will be all right if it was not in any medicine bundle."

This was the first piece of medicine equipment Klah owned, and he prized it as long as he lived, considering it powerful because it was so old.

They walked around to view the painted figures, and Klah bent his mind to memorizing the characters, their costumes, masks, and all the articles that were carried in the hands, along with the sequence of colors. He had seen the same figures in Yeibichai sand paintings, but these seemed more complete and more elaborately decorated. His uncle said, "Some medicine man who was afraid his ceremony would be forgotten spent much time in this cave, smoothing the walls and painting these figures. It may have been before the trip to the Bosque Redondo, and when he knew he would have to go, he brought his medicine bundles and all of the things he could not carry with him to hide in this cave. He built a wall to close the opening and then probably camouflaged it with loose rubble and brush, fully intending to recover them on his return; but he did not return."

"That may be the way it was," answered Klah, "or the medicine man who left these things may have thought he was leaving something for posterity, but, because he had not given them to anyone or told a relative where to find them, they were still his personal property, as surely as though they had been buried in the grave beside him. No Navaho would ever touch them and they would never again be used in a Yeibichai Ceremony."

"Let us build up the stones to cover the opening," his uncle suggested. "And we better not tell anyone about this cave, or we might be accused of handling a dead man's property." Klah shivered. He wanted nothing to do with black magic, and he was glad he had touched nothing around the bundles, but he never forgot the tall, painted figures of the immortals.

This Apache uncle was a medicine man who knew and held the Chizie-bin-la-Chizie or Apache Wind Chant. Although he sang this chant with Apache words, the language was so similar to the Navaho's that Klah had no difficulty understanding him. After attending some of these ceremonies with his uncle, Klah could assist with much of the detail of the rites and with the chanting. His uncle wanted him to study to become a wind chanter, but Klah thought he would soon be going to his own home, and he knew that memorizing a ceremony would take a long time. Still there would be no harm in learning some of it as long as he was here. And then an accident happened which caused him to stay much longer than he had expected.

While Klah was riding along the edge of a sandy arroyo, the bank gave way beneath the pony's feet and they both rolled down the bank to the floor of the arroyo. It was not very deep and the bottom was soft, but the pony's flying feet hit Klah several times. His collar bone was broken, two or three ribs cracked, and there was something seriously wrong with his hip which may have been a fractured pelvis. The pony scrambled to its feet and went home dragging its reins, and soon his uncle came searching for Klah. They carried him home, and a messenger was sent for the aunt who was a herb specialist. A brush shelter was built to serve as a hospital room, and in this she took care of him. With brews of tansy, yarrow, and boneset, she sought to stem his fever and ease the pain, while splints, poultices, and bandages held his arm to his side. The collar bone and the ribs healed quickly, but he still could not walk.

The Apache uncle made him a pair of ash-wood crutches with which to hobble about, but he stayed in the brush shelter as long as the aunt remained with him. It was during this period of invalidism that Klah was discovered to be a hermaphrodite. This accident of birth placed him in a very special category among his family and his contemporaries. The Navahos believed him to be honored by the gods and to possess unusual mental capacity combining both male and female attributes. He was expected to master all the knowledge, skill, and leadership of a man and also all of the skills, ability, and intuition of a woman. Klah during his lifetime lived up to these expectations in every way.

After Klah was able to walk on his crutches, his Apache uncle decided to hold a Wind Chant over him to complete his recovery. So all preparations were made, and Klah, being weary of inaction, helped collect the herbs, rewind and feather the prayer sticks, and paint the kewthawns.

The Wind Ceremony lasted five days and five nights. Of importance were four large sand paintings depicting the sun, the moon, the four Wind People, the cactus, lightning arrows, clouds, and many other symbols subject to the influence of the wind. When it had ended, Klah had memorized all of the prayers, the ritual, the body painting, and the sand paintings. All of this now belonged to him, and he could use it to hold a ceremony for a sick person if he wished. But Klah never sang the five-day chant; he chose the parts he considered the most powerful and condensed them into a three-day ceremony, which he was frequently called upon to use, mostly for coughs, sore throat, or chronic difficulty in breathing. On this side of the mountains he was not considered the best wind chanter. As long as his uncle lived and could hold the chant, Klah was just his neophyte and must pay the older man part of any remuneration he received.

After the Wind Ceremony, Klah still walked on crutches, so his uncle thought a Fire Ceremony, sometimes called the Knife Chant by the Navahos, might restore him to his former strength. The uncle did not know this ceremony, but there was an Apache medicine man living near Fort Defiance who did. This elderly Ahzayklin was a very primitive person with no learning outside of that of his own cult, so his rites were wild and somewhat barbarous. His chant lasted three nights, and all of the activities centered around the fire or a sand painting of the sun. Near morning of the third night, the fire was reduced to a bed of hot coals on which the medicine man placed four prehistoric stone spearheads—black obsidian on the east, gray (blue) flint on the south, yellow flint on the west, and pink agate on the north. There they were sterilized while a long prayer was intoned by the medicine man and repeated by the patient, then they were set aside till they were cool enough to handle.

After Klah had been given a ceremonial bath and dried with white cornmeal, the medicine man took one spearhead and quickly slashed a cross on one shoulder blade. A helper held a turtle-shell cup under it to catch the spurt of blood. Another spearhead was used for the other shoulder, and again the blood was saved. This process was repeated with the other two spearheads slashing crosses on his hips, from which blood was also taken. I do not know what became of this blood but hope it was not used to mix with powders and herbs to use as "medicine."

These open wounds, in the shape of crosses, each about one and one-half inches long, were then pinched together and held in place with pitch over which mutton tallow was spread. Klah evidently did not know that he was to be subject to such drastic treatment to let the evil spirits out of his body, and he did not approve of this way of doing it when the right prayers would have served just as well, but he endured the pain without flinching and carried the crossed scars all of his life.

This ceremony he seldom mentioned, and I would never have heard of it if I had not happened to see the scars on his shoulders. One afternoon, it was warm in his hogan, as he was burning bundles of herbs to make enough ashes for the "blackening" of some healing rite, and he had shed his shirt. As I entered the hogan, I saw the two shoulder scars and knew they must have been made during some ceremony, but although I had attended many rites of all kinds, I knew nothing of anything like this. He told me about the Apache medicine man and the Fire Ceremony, stressing the fact that the Navahos do not have as barbaric ceremonies as the Apaches. He said it was this kind of thing the Navahos had got away from when they separated from the Apaches to form a more peaceful nation.

They had divided their ceremonies, the Apaches taking the Sun Dance, the Boy's Initiation Ceremonies, the Scalp Dance, the Wind Chant, the War Dance, and the Devil Dance. The Navahos kept their own versions of some of these but practiced no bloodletting or self-torture. The early Navahos seem to have been in closer touch with the culture of the Puebloans than had the Apaches and had adopted more of the Pueblo religion, which included the elaborate and beautiful Peace Chants for healing and for blessing, while the Apaches clung to their more primitive rites.

Not long after this ceremony, Klah's uncle who sang the Hail Chant came to stay a few days to gather willow wands, lily roots, hollow cane grass, and bulrush pollen for ceremonial uses. It did not take long to collect all he could carry, and when he was ready to start for home, Klah packed his belongings, which now included many medicine articles his Apache uncle had given him, and accompanied him on the homeward journey. Klah's mother, Ahson Tsosie, had sent word for him to come home, for she needed his help with the shearing and marketing of the wool. Since he was now in his teens, he would be expected to fill a man's place in the family economy.

It was midsummer, and, since they had no need to hurry, the journey through the mountains was slow and pleasant. On the way, the two stopped often to pick berries or to gather the leaves and roots of some plant they thought the aunt could use. They made several short detours to visit with friends who were living in their summer homes among the spruce and piñon trees. So it was not long until word spread across the eastern mountainsides that Klah was on his way home, now an accredited Wind Chanter.

10. The Education of a Medicine Man

FOR A TIME, Klah was content to help his family with the lambing, shearing, planting, marketing, and other labors that filled the spring and early summer. Since these were often community projects, he was given opportunity to renew his friendships with the boys of his own age, learn of the events that had happened while he was away, and relate his own experiences. His training in ceremonial procedure made him talk and act more mature than the other boys, and he enjoyed better the conversation of the older men.

At night, after the family had gathered around the evening fire, it was customary for his uncle to sit in the place of honor and, when all were seated, to relate a legend or describe a rite that belonged to the Hail Ceremony. The younger generation listened carefully, for this was intended to be part of their education. He told of the first ceremonies used by his people, and he told of the immortals from whom they had been learned. He said, "In the early days there were five ceremonies which originated at one time. These were the Hail Chant, the Wind Chant, the Rain Chant, the Water Chant, and the Feather Chant. The time when all these were started was after the last Navaho flood [There are four in Navaho legend.], after all the monsters had been slain so the earth at last was safe for people to spread out and live in different places. Each one of these ceremonies was known and given by a different medicine man who seemed to have been living near one of the prehistoric pueblos now lying in ruins. These stone houses may have been inhabited when the first Navaho families arrived here, as the legend calls them 'the homes of the gods,' and the dwellers were the ceremonial instructors." It was a long story that took many evenings to complete.

The Hail Ceremony may have been learned from the "ancients" who lived at Pueblo Bonito before the drought conditions forced them to leave the Río Chaco. The legend tells of a poor family of wandering Navahos who built a crude hogan near this stream and came into contact with the Pueblo dwellers, whom they may have looked upon as "gods." The younger son of this Navaho family was the hero of this tale and eventually became the first Navaho medicine man to hold the Hail Chant. After the hero had erred by dallying with the wife of White Thunder, he was blasted and entirely disintegrated by the elements, as this story deals entirely with the elements—the thunder, the wind, the hail, rain, sleet, and snow.

The "gods" held a Hail Ceremony for him, and he was completely restored, as were all of his family and friends who had been killed in the battle with the elements. Four rites were held, so that the healing and resurrection came from four points of the compass, and the final benediction or Peace Ceremony came from above. The first four days of this chant were therefore placed in the category of "war ceremonies," as they were to cure injuries from the elements and from accidents and those incurred during war; but the fifth and last was a Peace Rite to overcome all effects of the illness and strife and to establish a whole spirit and peace of mind. Klah soon learned the legend of the Hail

Chant, a tale with a warp of history and a woof of colorful embellishment from generations of storytellers.

With the coming of warm weather, the Navahos of Tunicha Valley moved to the mountains, and Ahson Tsosie with all of her clan were again at Des-cheen-di-kana. Now was the time to card, spin, and dye wool for weaving rugs. Klah's sister, Ahdesbah, had become quite expert with the weaving implements and assisted her mother, turn and turn about, at the loom. Now that Klah was home, he also was expected to assist with this labor, and it was not long until he became as expert as his sister. With three weavers working on the same rug, it was not such a wearisome task, and they could complete a blanket and sell it with sufficient frequency to keep the family supplied with food through the "hunger" months before the harvest. These rugs were of very special weave, smooth and finely patterned, reflecting what Ahson Tsosie had learned from her Hopi relatives, who excelled in fine weaving and intricate design for ceremonial purposes. All weaving halted, however, when the Navaho families moved to the cornfields. There they were busy at other tasks, and the looms were taken down and stored in the hogans.

When the autumn ceremonial season arrived, Klah helped his uncle hold several Hail Chants, taking charge of more and more of the ritual, for his uncle's eyesight was failing. It was only by the sense of touch that the uncle could determine the difference between his prayer sticks and his feathered wands, and a helper always had to see that he had the correct sacks of pollen. As for the sand paintings, he instructed Klah in painting them on buckskin so they could be spread out for the sand painters to copy. In doing this for his uncle, Klah was able to memorize all aspects of this chant, and when many of the sketches were buried with the old chanter, Klah had them in mind.

At the end of the season, when winter had halted most of the ceremonial activities, this uncle decided he could no longer conduct a Hail Chant properly, and now that Klah had it well memorized, he would retire and his nephew could carry on. He gave Klah all of his medicine bundles, prayer sticks, rattles, and other equipment except the ones that contained his own spiritual magic, and these he kept to use occasionally and have buried with him when he died. However, no older medicine man is ever relegated to obscurity. He is still the possessor of spiritual power and knowledge which gains strength with the passing years. So it was not Klah who was contacted when a Hail Chant was desired —it was the older man, but always in Klah's presence. When the ceremony started, the old chanter was always there, enthroned on a roll of sheep pelts and blankets with his rattle, his little buckskin bags of pollen, his gish, and his prayer plumes. As Klah went through the ceremony, the uncle accompanied every rite and chant with voice and rattle, and when it was finished, he was the one who received payment in sheep or silver. This he promptly divided with Klah according to previous agreement.

Klah told of the first ceremony he held under the guidance of his uncle, but depending entirely on his own memory. The patient was a boy about nine years old who had been herding his family's flock of sheep in the foothills among scattered juniper and piñon trees when a heavy black cloud swept across the sky and rain came pelting down.

He herded the sheep under the widespreading branches of a cedar, and when it commenced to hail, he crawled under a tame ewe. Lightning struck the cedar tree, killing two of the sheep and knocking him unconscious. When the storm was over, his father found him and took him home. Although he regained consciousness and did not seem to be injured in any way, he could not talk. Of course, his parents thought that the hail, rain, and lightning spirits were angry with him and had taken away his speech as punishment for something he had done that did not please them.

They did not know which ceremony should be held to cure the child, so they called a well-known diagnostician to hold a trance rite to determine the best chant they could have. The medium told them to have a Hail Ceremony sung over the boy to propitiate the angry spirits, who would then restore his speech. Klah and his uncle were engaged to hold a five-day-and-night ceremony with all of the boy's relatives and friends as helpers. Klah brought the herbs, pollens, and medicine bundles, the uncle brought the prayer plumes, incense, and the fumigant. Three small sand paintings and four large ones depicting the Hail People, the Wind People, the Rain, the Clouds, Lightning, and the Rainbow were made. Prayers and pollen were offered these characters to gain their good will. The boy was given a herb infusion, sprinkled with pollen, and treated with the sacred medicine bundles. On the last day his body was painted with rainbow arcs and he was given incense to inhale. As he was leaving the ceremonial hogan, he spoke for the first time: "I am all right now, Yah-tah-hay."

After the uncle's death, Klah was the only chanter on the Reservation who knew the complete Hail Ceremony.

Others knew parts of it and could sing the prayer chants and make one or two sand paintings, but they could not carry through a whole ritual. Although it was an important healing rite much in demand for certain ailments, it was not one of the greatest, since it lasted only five days and nights. There were other ceremonies that required more knowledge of myth, prayer, and ritual that covered a period of nine days and nine nights. These were the Yeibichai, two forms of the Mountain Chant, the Feather Chant, and the Big-House Ceremony. Before the march to the Bosque Redondo there had been many more of equal or superior importance. The one that had been completely lost, which once was the greatest of all, was the Nah-hos-dzan-ji, or Mother Earth Blessing Chant. This was a very early ceremony and one of the few the Navaho people brought with them when they came to the Southwest. A small part of it is still known and used in the Tah-di-teen-ji or Pollen Chant, and some of its ritual is performed in all of the Peace Chants. The Water Chant was also one of the first to be held since it commemorated the receding of the water after the last flood. It was a major ceremony and lasted nine days, with many beautiful sand paintings and unusual rites. Now it was of five days' duration, known only to two chanters, and was seldom held.

The Rain Chant, called Nilth-tsa-baka-niha-ji, which had been a companion of the Hail Chant, had disappeared, but many of its rites, prayers, and sand paintings were now used in other ceremonies. Navaho ceremonialism never again reached the magnificence of the years before the coming of the white soldiers. Many other ceremonies had been abandoned and forgotten. Among them were the Tsa-ha-ji, or Awl Chant, and the Chil-a-shuzzie or Good Luck Dance in which the dancers painted their bodies with ashes, wore buckskin war bonnets, and danced with bows and arrows, shooting in every direction to frighten away the evil spirits. The Non-Jadi-baha-ji, or Antelope Dance, was given up when antelope ceased to be extensively hunted, and the Kay-nal-yeathi, or Shoes and Leggings Ceremony, was dropped when the Navahos gave up wrapping their legs with buckskin in the manner of the Puebloans and started wearing red deer-hide shoes. Now that wars were ended, there was no reason for holding the Bit-tsay-atzin, which was a ceremony for blessing the eagle feathers worn by the warriors. Thus the major ceremonies had narrowed down to five or six in number, and the others were shortened to five days, or three days, and some lasted only one night. With this abbreviation of ritual came the discarding of bulky and unwieldy equipment to the extent that medicine men were able to carry their ceremonial paraphernalia in saddlebags or blanket rolls.

Klah was not satisfied to close his study of ceremonial lore with the three chants he now knew. He would have liked to learn all of them, but there seems to have been a code established by precedent that limited his study to teachers who belonged to his mother's, his father's, or his grandmother's clans. This was no great restriction, for Narbona's large family had provided him with many great-uncles and aunts, among whose numerous children were to be found a wide variety of medicine men. I noted one unusual circumstance—all of these chanters were shamans of the cultural or Peace Chants, and none performed the War Chants, the Shooting Ceremony, or the Hochonji (evil-dispelling) Rites. The Apache Wind Chant can be classed in this last category, but it was Apache and not Navaho.

Many members of Klah's family held a conference to determine which of the major chants he should undertake to learn next. His grandmother's second husband had been named Hosteen Nez Begay and had lived at Giagas Wash near the base of Huerfano Peak. He and his brother, Bear Face, had been famous medicine men who sang the Mountain Chant, which was more commonly known as the Bear Ceremony because it was customary to lead a live bear cub through a certain part of the ritual. The brother had been trying to tame a good-sized bear cub to use in these rites when the bear turned on him and clawed a long chunk of flesh from one side of his face. The wound eventually healed, but there had been no flesh transplanted, and the skin had pulled back, leaving cheekbone and teeth exposed. I have this description from Richard (Dick) Simpson, who was an early trader and owned a post near this peak: "Hathile Bear Face was a terrible sight; children screamed when they saw him for the first time." But he lived for years, and the two brothers taught the Male Mountain Chant to two of their nephews who had become well-known medicine men. However, no one tried to include live bears in the ceremony, deciding that bears pictured in sand would serve the purpose just as well and not be half as dangerous. One of these nephews, Hathile Nez, had married Ahson Tsosie's cousin and asked that Klah come and live with them to learn this chant, the ceremony, and the myth.

He was eager to have three or four boys as neophytes so that his ceremony would not be lost when he grew old and because he could demand a good price from the parents of the boys for their training. Since the ceremony lasted nine days and nights, with hundreds of chants, many long prayers, and several elaborate sand paintings, it would take the boys three or four years to memorize it. To make the learning more difficult, it was held only in the fall after the bears had hibernated and was so expensive that few Navaho families could afford it; thus the boys did not have a chance to witness it often. The only way they could learn it was to live with the medicine man's family, listen to the "bear myth," and join in the prayer chants during the long winter evenings around the hogan fires. The sand paintings were taught to them, not in their complete forms, as that would bring bad luck when there was no ceremony in progress, but figure by figure and symbol by symbol, with the instruction, "This is for the center of the painting, and this figure is in the east," or "White is the color of the north and blue belongs in the south," or "The rainbow guards three sides, but the eastern opening is guarded by two bears."

And so, from November until March, Klah remained at the home of this medicine man, helping with the work wherever needed and giving his full attention to memorizing the Zilthkayji-bakaji, or Bear Chant.

Early in March, Klah strapped his bundled belongings to the back of his saddle and rode home to help with the spring work. His share of the family flock numbered now above one hundred sheep, and he owned several horses. Property rights, even those of babies and children, are strictly observed in any Navaho family, although payment is generally expected for any extra expenses. Klah's parents took a sheep now and then as payment for their care, and when the wool was sold, Klah paid for his own ceremonial education. He remained with his family all summer, for the mountain home among the trees was cool and pleasant. Again he helped his mother and sister with the weaving. He enjoyed forming the intricate designs, but he never attempted the carding or the spinning, which was strictly "women's work."

In late fall he returned to the home of Hathile Nez to to continue his studies, and again he remained until spring. During this time, the ceremony was held twice on different parts of the Reservation and the boy students helped with all of the small details. One of the other boys was older and stronger than Klah but was jealous of his ability to memorize the prayers and the hundreds of chants. He began to say mean things and to blame Klah for everything that went wrong. Klah was not timid, but he refused to quarrel with anyone, and the next fall he did not go back. He had studied long enough to memorize the entire ceremony but not long enough to earn any of the medicine articles belonging to this chant. He never made any attempt to collect the necessary parphernalia for these rites, and he never offered to act as helper to a medicine man who was holding this chant. Years later, however, when I asked him to relate the myth and the ritual and to help me in drawing the sand paintings, he went through the entire ceremony without hesitation; so he had not forgotten, even though twenty years had passed.

That fall, while attending a nine-day Yeibichai Ceremony at Crystal Springs, Klah became acquainted with the chanter, Hathile Nah-cloie, who was conducting the chant and who he discovered was a member of the Yei-ee-dinnae clan, which was the clan of his great-grandfather, Chief Narbona. They immediately traced a relationship, and Hathile

THE YEIBICHAI CEREMONIAL LODGE
used by Klah for His "graduation ceremony"

Scene at Klah's give away ceremony

Nah-cloie (Laughing Chanter) asked Klah if he would care to be his helper and study the Yeibichai Ceremony under his tutelage. Klah thought of the cave he had found in the Arizona cliffs and the figures of immortals he had seen painted on the walls. He thought that perhaps this discovery was an omen indicating that this was the ceremony he should choose for his life's work. His parents were pleased with his decision. Nah-cloie was a prominent and well-liked medicine man throughout the entire Reservation. He had gained his name because of his good nature and his pleasant expression. He was seldom angry, and even when he was did not vent his ire on those with whom he came in contact.

Nah-cloie was an old man now, growing stiff with rheumatism, and he needed a helper to assist him with his ceremonial rites. Several years before, he had worked with Washington Matthews, helping him assemble the material for a book called *The Night Chant* (Yeibichai). This book is still considered the most accurate account of a Navaho ceremony that has ever been published.

How many autumns Klah spent with the older medicine man in order to learn the ceremony, he did not say. But he could not spend as much time there as he had at other places because he was a man now with livestock that required his attention. But he continued to act as assistant to Laughing Chanter as long as the older man was able to conduct ceremonies. Even then, Klah did not believe that he was prepared to take over the role of head shaman for these rites, but served two autumns as assistant to Tall Chanter, who also was one of Washington Matthews' informants. Tall Chanter (Hathile Nezzi) was quite different in disposition from Hathile Nah-cloie. He was a tall, stern man who was easily displeased and sharply critical, but he was a perfectionist, very careful of every detail of his ritual and sand painting, and very exact in relating the story that explained his ceremony. This was just what Klah wanted, for he, too, desired to have every point correct. Tall Chanter's form of the Yeibichai was called the Tsitsonji Klayji, while that of the Laughing Chanter had been the Tse-neeji Klayji. There were different prayers and chants and different sets of sand paintings, but the ritual was carried through in the same manner.

There are five other forms of the Yeibichai Chant, but these two are the only ones still being practiced by the Navaho medicine men. Klah knew the Tohe-hanigi, the Tahditeenji, and the Nahseelit-b-haji, but these are forgotten now that Klah has gone. There was another called Hostji-tsosie, which was a ceremony to restore the "Stricken Twins," one of whom was blind and the other lame. Because this first ceremony was held in the Canyon de Chelly, so all following performances were held in the canyons. Klah never studied this form of the Yeibichai, but he knew the myth and the herb medicines that were used.

All together, Klah studied twenty-six years before holding his first Yeibichai as its leading chanter. But this did not mean he had completed his education on the subject. If he heard of any chanter who did the rites differently, he immediately went to him to learn his way and his songs and prayers. When he held his first ceremony, he asked all critics to watch for errors. As there were none, he was an accredited Yeibichai chanter, but it was not until 1917 that he attained his highest degree.

11. *Weaver and Medicine Man.*

THE FIRST RUG Klah ever wove completely by himself was the one he made in Chicago at the World's Columbian Exposition. In 1892–93, the Territory of New Mexico arranged an Indian exhibit as one of the main features of their display in their building at the Exposition. The man who collected the attractions to be exhibited and was responsible for their transportation and care while in Chicago did not wish to bother with women weavers. He arranged to take several Pueblo men and one woman potter, since no Pueblo men could make pottery. He found a Navaho silversmith and an elderly medicine man, then tried to find a Navaho man who could weave. Someone told him about Klah and he came to see him, and Klah was glad to go.

In the exhibit building, Klah was given a roped-off space for his loom and his yarns so that sight-seers could not crowd too close. Every day he wove a few inches when the visitors were watching, and then waited until the next day to weave more, as he wanted this one piece of weaving to last until the close of the Exposition. The rug was completed before the summer ended, and when it was taken from the loom, it was presented to Klah, although he had been paid for making it. On his return he gave it to his sister, who, in turn, gave it to one of her daughters, and I believe Mrs. Jim still has it.

In the book *Navajo Indians,* Dane and Mary Coolidge state that Klah (Tla) essayed his first weaving in 1893:

In a sealed cave in the Cabezon Mountains an explorer had discovered a very perfect ancient blanket made from the under wool of mountain sheep. It was to copy this blanket that Klah set up a loom in a secret place and laid in a supply of red, brown, and white wool to match the original. He borrowed the precious relic for one-half day, in which time he wove another exactly like it.

I have heard the story of this rug several times, and I believe Dane Coolidge's interpreter did not give him the correct interpretation. For one thing, Klah had long since gained the reputation of being an excellent weaver, as he had been weaving ordinary rugs most of his life. This one was, more than likely, the first one of ancient design he had ever tried. But no novice at weaving could have followed the intricate pattern or used the fine yarn necessary to reproduce this relic. Another factor is the time in which the weaving was accomplished. He probably did borrow the original for one-half day, and in that time he matched his yarns, examined the warp, and memorized every detail of the design. As for weaving a rug in half a day, I am sure it would be physically impossible, for it takes minutes to pass the shuttle back and forth just once and more minutes to tamp the yarn into place, and no one can hurry the process. Also, there was no reason for Klah to work in secret, since everyone knew he was a weaver and this was not a ceremonial rug. But if this blanket had been found wrapped around a skeleton, then handling it would be strictly taboo and owning it would class the owner as a grave robber, although weaving a copy would carry no penalty.

In 1910 Klah copied a rug fragment that had been found in Chaco Canyon by the Hyde Expedition. At this time they asked him to make just a segment to indicate what the colors and design might have been before it was stained by the clay in which it had been buried. He made a small rug of a design similar to the section they had sent. In 1915 the curator of the museum wrote my husband, Arthur, asking if he could find someone to weave a large blanket the same size as the original before it crumbled in the dirt. Klah and his sister agreed to attempt a duplicate. We furnished the wool which Grandma Klah carded and spun almost as fine as linen thread. Then Ahdesbah dyed the yarn with specially made Du Pont dyes trying to prepare enough to make a whole rug, as it is almost impossible to obtain the same colors at a second dyeing. It took them all summer. The finished product was nine by eleven feet and contained three shades of red and pink, two shades of soft green, delft blue, white, black, brown, and gray. I believe this blanket may still be seen in a Boston museum.

The next year Klah made a blanket showing a set of Yeibichai dancers, which he sold to Mr. Ed Davies for several sheep. When other medicine men and Navahos found out about this rug, there was quite a furor, and they demanded that Klah hold an "evil-expelling" rite and that the rug be destroyed. But the trader told them he was sending it to Washington and that it would be hung on a wall where it would not be walked on. When the rug was off the Reservation, the excitement subsided and the incident was forgotten.

When Arthur bought the Pesh-do-clish trading post in 1913 and went there to learn the business, Klah was one of the first Indians with whom he became acquainted. Mr. Nelson, the former owner, stayed a few weeks to collect whatever outstanding debts he could, and then went to his farm on the San Juan River. Arthur's brother, Earle, stayed with him part of the time and added a kitchen, porch, bedroom, and closet to the original two rooms which had been the living accommodations. But Earle was away much of the time and Arthur was alone, so Klah came in the afternoons and spent many long evenings helping him with his study of the Navaho language. Klah was generally invited to stay for the evening meal, then the two would sit by the fireplace while Arthur wrote lists of nouns and phrases which he would carry in his shirt pocket for days, until he was sure he would not forget. The Navahos told me that Klah had taken Arthur into his clan as a nephew, but I doubt that any rite was ever held. However, a strong bond of friendship was established that lasted as long as Klah lived and which included me as well.

When my school year ended in June, 1914, Arthur came to Fort Defiance, where I had been teaching, and we were married on June 30, going to Pesh-do-clish the same day. The first Navaho who came into our living room to greet the new bride was Hosteen Klah. How he knew that a gift was in order, I do not know, for it is not customary for Navahos to present gifts to the bride, but he brought me the most beautiful untanned fox pelt I had ever seen then or since. It was all gold and white, with only a spot of black on the tip of the tail and a black nose. I sent it to Denver where it was made into a beautiful stole which I was proud to wear for many years.

We were new at the trading business and too deeply in debt to carry a large amount of trade goods. But Klah came to trade with us, bringing his family and his friends and warning us against grafters. He always knew when cere-

116

monies were to be held in our vicinity and advised Arthur
of the extra goods we should have in stock to meet the de-
mands of the many people. At this time, there were four or
five wealthy Navaho families within a ten- or fifteen-mile
radius of our post. Hosteen Bichai was the oldest and
owned the most sheep. Klah and his family came next, with
about 2,500 head of sheep and goats and 60 or 70 head of
cattle. He never was sure how many horses there were, since
all of the horse herds pastured together and were separated only at branding time or when another horse was
needed by some member of the family. He did not spend
much time with his sheep except at lambing or shearing
season, since he was much in demand to preside at healing ceremonies for many miles around. His mother, his sister,
and three nieces, together with two or three adopted orphan
boys, seemed to keep the flocks cared for.

Whenever he heard of a Navaho medicine man who
he thought might know a few prayers or rites unknown
to him, he would go to the man's home and stay a week
or ten days, even though he lived a hundred or more miles
away. In the spring of 1917, when he was forty-nine years
old, he told Arthur that he had conferred with and com-
pared ceremonies with every Yeibichai chanter in the Navaho tribe—there were none he had not contacted. He had
learned something from each one, and now there was nothing more for him to learn. He said, "This fall I will hold the
greatest Yeibichai that has ever been held on the Reservation since before the Navajos were taken to the Bosque Redondo, and I will ask everyone to come and criticize. If
there is any mistake or omission, I will start studying all
over again."

117

All summer long he planned the great ceremony and made preparations for it, since it was to be his final graduation as an unsurpassed Yeibichai medicine man. Men with teams and wagons were hired to go to the mountains to bring trees and branches that would be used to build the brush shelters for the dancers and the cookhouse. Other wagons brought long logs and poles for the construction of the ceremonial lodge. The Black Rock Spring, which sent forth a small creek and ordinarily furnished enough water for family and stock, would not be sufficient for the hundreds of horses that would need water or for the Navahos who would be camping near. Going half a mile down the valley, he marked a place for a dirt dam and then hired men with teams and scrapers to hollow out a wide space above it, using the dirt to construct a long, six- or seven-foot-high embankment. After the summer rains, this held a wide, shallow lake which, being new, was free of quicksand. So now, although there were no trees or lakes in the valley, he had both wood and water for any number of people and for every purpose.

There were many other things he would need, and he asked to see our merchandise catalogs. Although he could not read, nearly everything he desired was pictured, and he spent several afternoons making his selections, marking articles on page after page. Three beautiful hand-tooled saddles, ten all-wool Pendleton shawls, bolts of calico and sateen, shoes for the younger generation, cases of tomatoes, peaches, coffee, crackers, and sacks of sugar and flour—Arthur was told to order all of this and have it ready in time for the ceremony, which was to be held the first week in October, as soon as Klah had sold his sheep.

When the date was finally determined, invitations were sent in every direction and Klah sent special messengers to the governors of the Zuñi, the Jemez, the Laguna, and the Hopi pueblos, saying that if any of their people wished to come, they would be welcome and would be considered as guests of honor, especially their medicine men. All of these Pueblos sent representatives, who were taken into the ceremonial lodge and given "red carpet" treatment.

Finally the sheep were sold, and all of the goods had arrived, and were safely stored in our warerooms. The large ceremonial lodge was ready, and the brush cookhouse and other brush shelters had been erected. Then the Navahos began to arrive. There had been a small army of men to do the building, and now came the clan families who would help to pay for the ceremony and the older women who would spend their days making and baking bread in the newly constructed adobe ovens. There were the families who would slaughter the sheep and cattle and handle the barbecue fires; they built their own shelters where they could manage the herds. There was much excitement and dashing about as each group found a satisfactory place to camp and settle down for a nine-day stay.

On the opening day there were dozens of family groups around canvas-covered wagons stationed a little distance from the ceremonial grounds. These wagons would be used as sleeping quarters for the women and the children and headquarters for their men. Hundreds of Navahos had come on horseback, and they too established camping places on the mesa. Day by day the attendance increased until, on the morning of the ninth day, there may have been five hundred wagons and well over two thousand Navahos. Such a vast assembly had not been brought together since the government had collected them for the trip to the Bosque Redondo.

There was no sick patient for the ceremony, as Klah was giving it to demonstrate his knowledge and ability as a medicine man. His sister took the part of "patient," although she was perfectly well. This fact did not deter others from receiving treatment at this time if they wished and were willing to pay something toward defraying the expenses. One family with a daughter who had trachoma gave a yearling steer, several others brought sheep, while some earned treatment by helping with the chores. The Yeibichai Ceremony was thought to cure eye trouble, and, as many Navahos had trachoma, there were several patients.

During the first five days, the rites were held at long-spaced intervals. To attend these, I kept my pony saddled and was ready to go with no delay, for I knew they would wait for me to arrive.

At night there was practice dancing, a boy's and young men's chorus around a bonfire, and small purification rites with prayer chanting in the ceremonial lodge. Klah was seldom seen, since he occupied the place of honor in the lodge and from there issued his commands. He had told me that the first large sand painting would be made on the fifth day, starting early in the morning. Since I did not wish to miss any part of this activity, we breakfasted by lamp light, and as soon as the sun was up, I was on my way to the ceremonial lodge. As I pushed aside the door blanket and stepped over the threshold into the cool dimness of the interior, I realized the room was much larger than it had seemed from the outside. The floor space was circular and about eighteen feet in diameter, with a fire pit toward the east about three feet from the door.

Klah sat in the place of honor at the southwest, surrounded by an amazing number of pollen bags, prayer plumes, and rattles, while a large assortment of medicine bundles were piled against the west wall. Twelve or more chanters were seated or sprawled along the south, while two messenger boys squatted near the door. I handed Klah a polished abalone shell and a package of cigarettes, these being the customary ceremonial gifts, and then passed a package of cigarettes to the men. Klah motioned me to the northwest "corner," where a couple of saddle blankets had been folded for a seat. I carried a Navaho shawl, as I knew that Navaho women never exposed their ankles and I was afraid I could not sit with my feet folded under me during the entire proceedings. Someone questioned my presence in the lodge and was answered by Klah's nephew, but I understood very little Navaho at that time, so sat as quietly as I could.

Four men carrying blankets filled with clean adobe-colored sand from the bank of the arroyo entered the lodge, and emptied part of the contents on the floor at the center of the hogan, reserving part of it for future use. To the north of the door, a blanket had been spread on which a large grinding stone and a metate had been placed, along with sands and rocks of different colors. Benullie Begay was busy grinding the sands which would be used as dry paint to provide colors for the sand painting. There was white, red, and yellow sandstone; there was black charcoal to be ground with sand to make it heavy enough to fall through the fingers; and there was the charred root of the rock oak which would be ground with white sand to produce a beautiful pastel blue. Other colors such as brown, pink, or gray would be made by mixing two or three of the others. As each color was ground, a pile was placed on a slab of pine bark and each painter was given six different slabs of bark. There were five painters at the start, but they would alternate with others before the painting was completed, since nearly every Navaho in the hogan was an expert sand painter.

The design of this first large Yeibichai picture was called the "Whirling Log Sand Painting" and has become one of the best known of all the hundreds that are made for Navaho ceremonies. After the sand had been passed to the painters, two men used long weaving batons to smooth the center pile to a smooth mat for the background. Klah opened a sack of pollen and blessed all of the sand that would be used that day; then someone handed him a long cord, which was held across the background sand, first from east to west and then from north to south. This, snapped into the sand to make crossed lines, located the center. Klah took black sand to make a small black lake in this center which he bordered with white to represent foam, yellow for pollen, blue for summer rain, and red for sunlight. He then returned to his place and the five painters continued the design. Four black logs pointed in the four directions, while the four sacred plants, corn, beans, squash, and tobacco, were laid in the quadrants. At the east stood Hastje-altai, the teacher; at the west stood Hastje-hogan, the god of reproduction; on the north and on the south were the Bighones-kidi—the seed gatherers, bearers, and guards. A rainbow arc was painted to protect three sides, but the eastern side was open, with no guardian symbols.

With the painting finished, there was a pause for smokes and conversation. During this intermission, a file of women entered the lodge bringing big bowls of mutton stew, baskets heaped with small loaves of crusty bread that had been baked in the outdoor ovens, steaming black coffeepots, canned milk, sugar, and cookies, and cups and spoons. I wondered how the men would manage without plates, knives, or forks, but I soon found out. Every man had his own knife with which he carved off half a loaf of bread, then breaking this in two, he used the crusts to dip up the gravy, potatoes, and chunks of meat. The women poured the coffee and then retired to enjoy their own lunch hour. An hour or so later, at some signal from the medicine lodge, they returned to remove the empty baskets, bowls, and pots, which now were minus every scrap of food, as leftovers would have been an insult to the cooks.

As the men settled comfortably against the wall, Klah started waving his rattle, and when the correct rhythm had been reached, the chant began and continued for several minutes. Then, laying the rattle aside, he picked up his buckskin bag of pollen and, stepping carefully between the designs, sprinkled sacred pollen accompanied by prayer over each figure, then around on the rainbow, and, lastly, up through the opening in the roof. Twelve prayer sticks had been erected around the outside of the sand painting, and these, too, were blessed. With this blessing the picture became a sacred altar containing the spiritual power of the immortals.

There was no more talking or joking, no smoking or moving about. A crier stepped outside the door and called,

"The ceremony is about to begin. Hasten!" The patient was prepared and waiting and now entered the lodge followed by ten or twelve women of her family, who seated themselves along the wall while the patient still stood near the door. She was dressed in new clothing and a new Pendleton shawl. In the bend of her arm she carried a ceremonial basket filled with yellow corn meal. At a motion from the medicine man she walked near the painting and tossed a spray of corn meal on each figure as her gift to the immortal it depicted. Then she placed her shawl in the southeast corner and on it her silver beads, her velvet blouse, and her shoes and stockings, after which Klah led her onto the sand painting and motioned for her to sit on the western log facing the east.

The ceremonial rites consisted of pollen blessings, pressing of prayer bundles to her head and body, drinking of herb infusions, and face painting, these acts being separated by intervals of prayer chant. Near the close of these rites, the medicine man stepped onto the sand painting, pressed his moistened hands to the heads of all the sand figures, then pressed this sand to the patient's head. Then his hands were pressed to the shoulders of the figures and this sand was transferred to the shoulders of the patient. This continued down her body to her feet, so that the power of the sand-painted figures was transferred to the patient. Since these figures had been perfect, she would now gain perfect health. The last ceremonial rite was that of fumigation. Live coals from the fire pit were placed in front of the patient (and also in front of any member of the audience who wished to have them) and sprinkled with a mixture of herbs which included mint, sage, aromatic sumac, and several others. A dense blue aromatic smoke rose to cover the patient's face and be inhaled. This was to clear her mind of all fear of a repetition of the illness that had troubled her. When the smoke settled, a little water was thrown on the coals and the ceremony was over.

Klah held out a feather wand to help the patient to her feet, and she stepped off the painting to her shawl, gathered everything in her arms, and left the lodge, followed by the other women. The figures on the painting were badly blurred, and Klah now took a wand and erased every vestige of the design. When it was just a gray mat, the helpers scraped the sand into the carrying blankets and took it to the north, emptying it under the lee of a bank where it would not be walked on by sheep or cattle. I asked Klah if he ever kept the sand to use the next day, and he said "No! This has served its purpose and is still holy. It is part of the earth, and the winds will take it back to the place it belongs."

The next three forenoons I spent in the lodge watching the painters, under Klah's direction, complete three more beautiful and complicated sand altars, and on each occasion I did my best to memorize as many of the symbols as I could. Since pencil, paper, or camera was not allowed in the lodge, I had only my memory to depend on. But when the rites had ended and I had time to try putting these designs on paper, I found that my mental pictures were a jumble of rainbows, crossed logs, tall corn, and medicine bags. In later years I trained myself to concentrate, and if allowed to remain in a ceremonial hogan for a half-hour, I could reproduce the painting without an error.

When Klah saw me at the hopeless task of drawing these

first sand paintings, he asked if I would like to have him paint them for me. I was delighted and started looking for material of a quality that would last on which the paintings could be made. The heavy wrapping paper we used for wrapping rugs for shipment through the mails was just the right sand color, of good weight and with a smooth texture to serve as the background, So from this I cut four twenty-inch squares. I had a water-color painting outfit, and we obtained children's colored pencils from the store. Klah worked with the pencils and I with the paints. When two figures were alike, he drew one and I copied it for the other. He made the intricate designs and I drew the rainbows and the plants. It took a couple of weeks of our spare time, but finally I had my first four sketches of Navaho sand paintings, which number grew to be almost five hundred in the next twenty years.

How little one realizes that a small start often brings very important results that may affect many people's lives. When Klah saw how pleased I was with the sketches, he informed me there were several more that could be used in the Yeibichai Ceremony to cure different sicknesses, and that he knew them all. I prepared more material, and, as the year passed, he drew twelve more beautiful sand paintings belonging to the one chant. Then I attended an Apache Wind Chant he was holding over a woman with asthma and witnessed two paintings made for that ceremony, and later Klah helped me draw these and added two I had not seen. In late summer he held a five-day Hail Chant for a family whose child had been injured in a hailstorm. There were four large paintings used in this ceremony, as beautiful and complicated as any that had been made for the Yeibichai. Again we worked with our pencils, paints, and paper to make a record of these, and again Klah added two or three I had not seen. By this time, I had written many of the descriptions of the symbols with the names of the immortals and the powers they were thought to possess.

Recording Navaho symbolism was a project no white person had ever been able to undertake throughout any wide area of the Navaho country, but now I was visiting ceremony after ceremony and recording the sand paintings wherever the medicine man permitted. Soon my collection of sketches and other ceremonial artifacts attracted the attention of interested visitors to the Southwest, among them Wendell T. Bush of Columbia University. He stayed with us two days and visited a small ceremony, becoming quite interested in Navaho religion. On his return to New York City, he obtained a research grant for me and also purchased copies of thirty sand-painting sketches to display in the museum which bears his name.

Another eastern visitor was Mary Cabot Wheelwright, who was not interested at first; but after returning to visit us three or four autumns to attend the Navaho ceremonies and realizing that my collection was unique, she remarked, "This should be in a museum where it will be safe and where people can see it." Later she built the Museum of Navajo Ceremonial Arts in Santa Fe, where a great many of my sand paintings are on display.

12. Klah's Graduation Ceremony

Among the reservation Navahos, late autumn is the only time when the economic pressure of obtaining food for families and flocks does not occupy their entire time and effort. But when the corn has reached the roasting-ear stage and the sheep have fattened on the grass after summer rains, the Dinnae can take time to relax and turn their attention to ceremonies and social obligations. Everyone is ready to leave their hogans and their flocks to the care of the old folks, pack their wagons, saddle their best horses, and be on their way to some community gathering, large or small as the case may be. Distance seems to trouble no one, or the condition of roads and trails. There is always a path up the steepest mountain or some way of crossing the deepest arroyo.

Klah had sent blanket invitations to every Navaho community stating the time and purpose of his ceremony several weeks ahead of the actual date so that those living at a distance would have time to prepare for the trip. This included all members of the family who would travel, and few were willing to stay at home. The ostensible reason for attending was the obvious one of witnessing the ceremony to pass judgment on the correctness of the rites. But this was of interest only to the older people who were informed on Yeibichai procedure; the majority were eager to attend for reasons important only to themselves.

Such a vast assembly of persons was, in itself, a great social event, and many went just to see and be seen in order to establish a higher degree of social standing. Clan members and relatives who had not met for several years gathered in groups to get caught up on personal histories; crops and prices were discussed, weddings described, births and deaths enumerated. There were salesmen who took this opportunity to exhibit their goods. A silversmith carried a number of silver rings and bracelets about showing them to different groups, eventually disposing of all he had and receiving orders for many more. A man with a horse to sell loudly asked for bidders, and another announced the loss of a saddle and offered a reward for its return. Mothers with marriageable daughters quietly made contact with the mothers of marriageable sons, always with an eye to selecting a prominent family.

In the afternoons, when there were no ceremonial rites until sunset, people rested and amused themselves with games and sports. Men gathered in groups to play cards while their women played a game with flat sticks, all of them games of chance with bets placed on the outcome. Betting is a tribal pastime, and a Navaho will bet all of his possessions, even the silver buttons from his shirt. The sport which attracted the largest audience each afternoon was the horse racing. Across the flat, south of our post, Arthur had persuaded the highway maintenance crew to run their scraper up and down a half-mile stretch. The result was a smooth adobe race track that almost paralleled the highway.

Navahos who owned race horses often came from some distance to use this as a training track or for matched races, and even before the ceremony started, they arrived with their fastest horses. There had been racing every day, but we had been too busy in the store to take time to attend. However, on the sixth day, I decided to enter my saddle pony as one of the contestants. Bay Billy was a stocky Colorado cow pony, somewhat larger than the average Navaho horse and fast for a short distance. I had him saddled and rode him to the race track where several jockeys were walking their racers up and down the course. Jim Velieto, then a slim lad about fifteen years of age, was standing in the crowd, and I asked him to be my jockey. He was delighted, and, as I dismounted, he removed his shoes and coat, took the saddle off the pony's back, and strapped the surcingle tight to hold the saddle blanket in place. All horses were ridden without saddles or spurs, and Bay Billy never needed a quirt. The surcingle straps were looped at the sides to form stirrups, and the bridles had ordinary bits with no blinders at the sides.

On one side of the race track stood a hundred or more Navahos from our valley, and on the other side were the same number from other sections of the Reservation. Jim rode onto the track between the two groups and paced his horse slowly up and down the course. Everyone eyed Bay Billy, commenting on his good points and pointing out his weak ones, trying to estimate his speed. A horse owner from the opposite group led out a long-limbed, Roman-nosed gray gelding ridden by a small barefoot boy. The owner was Kee Becenti from Tohatchi and the rider was his son. I thought the horse looked like a veteran racer, and the boy seemed part of the horse—a hard combination to beat. Both horses were now paraded up and down the track for all to see and make a choice.

A blanket was spread on the track between the two

groups of spectators and the betting began. A person on one side would hold up a silver bracelet, which would be matched by a bracelet from the other side, then both would be deposited on the blanket. A silver bow guard might be matched with a string of white shell beads, and a silver belt buckle with a turquoise ring. A handful of silver buttons matched a hand-braided quirt. Gradually the number of articles on the blanket grew to a good-sized pile. I held up three silver dollars, and a woman on the other side matched with a pair of turquoise earrings. We both walked to the blanket and deposited our bets.

Finally the betting ended, and men on the racing committee knotted the corners of the blanket and set it to one side. The horses were ridden to the starting line, which was merely a line drawn in the dirt, and the starter raised his hat. Bay Billy stood quietly, but the gray made two false starts and was hard to hold; he was so nervous that I thought we might have a good chance of winning the quarter-mile dash. Then down came the hat and the horses were off with Bay Billy a half-length in the lead. All the riders needed to do was to bend low and hang on, as both animals knew what was expected of them. Gradually the gray crept up to Billy's shoulders and then to his neck, and at the finish line was definitely in the lead. The Navahos are good losers, and not a word was said or a complaint made when the blanket of bets was opened on the other side and its contents distributed to the winners.

Bay Billy had refused to halt at the finish line and ran to the end of the half-mile course; from there Jim walked him slowly back. Three other races were called in the meantime with half an hour between races for the placing of bets.

131

I asked Jim if he would like to try once more, and he said he would, for he thought he could do better this time. So he entered the fifth race and again walked the horse up and down the track waiting for a contestant. A slim sorrel belonging to Tod-di-cheeni of Coyote Canyon was ridden onto the track, and now the betting was heavy, as the audience had more than doubled and the horses seemed evenly matched. I held up four silver dollars, which were matched by a man on the other side, and we went to the blanket and laid down the money.

When the blanket of bets was taken away, the boys rode to the starting line and the noisy crowd became quiet as they waited for the signal from the starter. Bay Billy was prancing and sweating under his blanket while the sorrel, ridden by a twelve-year-old boy, was tossing his head and stepping sideways. When their noses were at the starting line, the hat was dropped and again Bay Billy jumped into the lead. The little sorrel was fast and drew ahead at the halfway mark, but lacked the stamina to hold her gain and was a length behind at the finish. The betters on our side burst into exclamations of joy, and the blanket was brought to our side to be opened and divided. I was handed eight silver dollars, and, going to where Jim was holding Bay Billy, I gave him four of the coins, then walking to the other side, I gave the remaining four to the boy who had ridden the sorrel. When I came back, Jim had the saddle on Bay Billy and I rode slowly to the post.

On the next to last day, the eighth of ceremonial procedure, a car stopped in front of the post and a man dressed in khaki came into the store. He was Walter Fewkes of the Smithsonian Institution in Washington, D.C., who was on his way to visit the ruins at Mesa Verde. He had seen the crowd of Navahos at the race track and had stopped for a moment to watch the races. He was very much interested in the Indians, and when Arthur told him there was a ceremony in progress, he asked if he might stay with us until it ended. We had no guest accommodations, but Arthur told him that if he could manage with a studio couch in the living room, he was welcome to stay. He replied that he would not be using it much anyway, for he planned to watch the rites held at night, but he would like to have his meals with us. We had another horse brought up and saddled for his use, for there was no way for his car to cross a deep arroyo.

I think Walter Fewkes was far more aware of the significance of the rites he witnessed than I was at the time. This was my first attendance at a major ceremony, and the color, noise, smells, and movement melted into one vast pageant that was quite overwhelming. The ninth day with its crowds of brightly dressed men and women, the rush and activity of thronging youth, and the clouds of dust from horses galloping about defied description. There were a few white people mingling with the swarms of Navahos; they were the traders' families and other friends Klah had invited to witness his graduation as a medicine man.

He had given orders for us to be admitted to the ceremonial hogan, where there were rolls of blankets to serve as seats. We were treated with courtesy, but we were not important or at all necessary. Many of the visiting Navahos resented our presence, but Klah was glad to have us attend and he was in command. Never have I witnessed a more completely Navaho festival. All of the people in charge were

Navahos, the wagons that brought fruit and melons from the San Juan River were Navaho wagons, and the salesmen were Navahos. Even the policeman, who came from the agency at Shiprock to display his bright new badge, was a Navaho. I am sure that this ceremony was the equal of those held in the days of Narbona's chieftancy when the Navaho people were called "The Lords of the Soil."

The weather throughout had been beautiful, with warm sunny days and cool sparkling nights. On the ninth morning there was stir and activity long before the sun peeped above the horizon. This was the big day when Klah would make his grand gesture of giving away his worldly wealth in order to devote his time and thoughts to things of a spiritual nature. In the ceremonial lodge, the sand painting was spread at sunrise in order to complete the healing rites before the noon hour, and the midday meal was eaten and hastily cleared away. Everyone wished to be ready for the "give-away" rites that would occupy most of the afternoon.

One of the family hogans had been emptied of personal belongings, and the floor was now stacked with new merchandise. In the center a ceremonial fire was barely flickering, and around the west and north walls chanters were sitting, waving their rattles and intoning ancient supplications to the Spirits of Peace and Plenty. On the floor two blankets had been spread, one to the north of the fire, the other to the south. Here the visitors came to bestow their gifts, one blanket holding gifts for the young men and the other for the maidens. Arthur had given me a paper sack containing quarters, and now I knew the purpose of these coins. The visitors in the hogans were tossing coins onto the blanket at the south and lengths of new calico onto the blanket at the north. I divided my quarters between the two, then stood with my back against the wall while many Navahos came and went.

After a time Klah arose and blessed the offerings with sacred corn pollen, after which he tied the coins into small pieces of cloth with perhaps two dollars in each package. While he had been doing this, boys had formed a triple line just outside the door and were chanting a series of traditional songs. Klah stood just west of the opening in the roof and tossed out the little moneybags, one by one, so that they would fall among the chanters. As a boy received a sack (and there was much scrambling), he would fall out of line so that another boy could secure the next one. When all had been tossed through the opening, a man came in to say that three of the boys had not received one. Klah opened his buckskin purse and filled three more little bags, which were taken to the boys outside.

When the chanting in the hogan was resumed, about an equal number of girls lined up in the same formation outside the door and began their ceremonial chant, each waving a sprig of spruce and swaying back and forth to the rhythm of the chant. Klah and a helper gathered up the rolls of cloth, draping them across their shoulders and around their necks in order to carry all of the pieces. When they stepped out of the door, the chanting stopped and there was an expectant hush as a piece of cloth long enough to make a full skirt was draped around the neck of each maiden, followed by a shorter piece of velveteen to make a blouse. There was some cloth left over, and Klah sent it to the women who were working in the cook-hogan. Twelve new Pendleton shawls were blessed and given to the older women who had helped cook and serve the food to the men in the ceremonial lodge. The three hand-tooled saddles were presented to the relatives who had furnished cattle and sheep for the feasts. Sheep were given to the men who made sand paintings, the dancers, and those who took part in the masked rites. A large carton filled with sacks of Duke's Mixture and Bull Durham tobacco was circulated among the men, and for the women and children there was an equally large carton filled with small sacks of mixed candies. No one was forgotten, and it seemed to me that the line of recipients was endless. With all this dispersal Klah still did not become a poor man. He had reserved for himself the sheep, cattle, and horses he would later divide among his nieces and their families, and there were still the hundreds of sheep belonging to his sister and to his mother, along with the greater number of his cattle and ponies.

As soon as the sun had set, families began bringing their blankets and food to pre-empt places near the dance arena where they could spend the night watching the dancers. I had been among the first and had been lucky in securing almost a ringside seat, where I placed cushions and blankets for the four in our party and a basket of sandwiches and a Thermos of hot coffee to furnish a midnight snack. All around us the Navaho families were tending small fires over which they roasted slivers of mutton and warmed their coffee while corncakes, wrapped in husks, toasted in the ashes. In the brisk night air carrying a minty tang from the spruce and piñon fires and the tantalizing aroma of roasting corn, grilled mutton, and black coffee, I defy the most finicky epicure not to develop a good healthy appetite. Anyway, it was just as well to come prepared.

It was not exactly a comfortable night, but it certainly was most interesting. I found the audience almost as intriguing as the ceremony, for these Navahos were of every type imaginable, some being tall and thin with hawklike features and others wide and fat with Eskimo faces. No two faces were alike, and no distinct racial feature was evident. There was one characteristic which remained constant —the babies all looked fat and healthy, with solemn faces and round, inquiring eyes. As we settled into our crowded quarters, elbow to elbow with beshawled women and blanketed men, we could hear the "woo-hoo-hoo" of the dancers who were being painted and costumed in the brush shelters to the east. Presently everyone became still, and the medicine man (Klah) came with two masked assistants to bless the dance arena. Shortly afterwards the first set of dancers appeared, and they, too, were blessed.

There were six men in the dance team, all dressed alike, their bodies painted white, woven dance kilts belted around their waists with blue fox pelts dangling at the back. All wore blue masks and spruce neckpieces, and all wore red deer-hide shoes. Each carried a gourd rattle in his right hand and a spruce twig in the left. These six were followed by the clown, Tohni-nili, who was costumed in the same manner but overdecorated with sprigs of spruce. He carried a small water pot and, running alongside the six dancers, occassionally sprinkled one with a few drops.

They started their chant in unison, each man tapping the earth with one foot until the rhythm had been established, and then they broke into a ritualistic dance that probably was as old as the tribe itself. When this team of dancers departed, another team was waiting to take its place, dressed exactly like the first, chanting the same prayers, and dancing the same routine. After these, still another team came on the dance field, followed by still another, and so on throughout the entire night. They were so nearly alike that I thought one team, or perhaps two, had performed all the dances. Later I learned that these were all different teams that had come from different parts of the Reservation to compete for prizes, the winning team receiving two sheep apiece, the second team receiving one sheep each. One group had brought their best dancers from Rainbow Mesa in Arizona and another had come from the Mancos River Valley in Colorado. There was a very good "home team" for whom I had supplied tiny sleigh bells to sew along the edges of their dancing kilts, and there were ten or twelve teams from other localities.

This exhibition may have been monotonous to the white visitors, but it was quite exciting to the Navaho audience. The judges sat near the upper end of the dancing floor and discussed each performance as it ended. How they could tell any difference was a mystery to me, as I thought each set perfect. A team from Lukachukai won the first prize, and our home team won second place. Ten years later, under Klah's tutelage, I was able to sit among the judges and have my opinions listened to with respect. Just as the first dawn-light was appearing in the east, the dancers all came on the dance floor, the medicine man came to the door of the ceremonial lodge, and the entire audience stood up and faced the east while the medicine men, chanters, and dancers sang the greeting to the new day. This was the "Blue-bird Song"—"*Dolie-ah-nee, Dolie-ah-nee*"—"The Bluebird comes, the Bluebird comes." It was the most impressive scene I have ever witnessed. A thousand soft-voiced Indians standing to face the east and greet the new day with a chanted prayer!

As the chant ended and the sun's rays swept the mesa, the women began gathering up their sleeping babies, their blankets, and other belongings to carry them to the wagons, and soon we heard the rattle of harness and the complaining squeal of wagon wheels. In a surprisingly short time, the space around the arena was deserted and the multitude of guests fading away in clouds of dust. The great ceremony was finished, but it had accomplished its purpose and would live long in the memories of all who had attended. It had cost Klah one-third of his wealth, but it had established his standing as the greatest Yeibichai chanter on the Navaho Reservation, and it also had spread his fame to the farthest reaches of Navaho country. From now on, he would not need to depend on sheep for his livelihood for his healing ceremonies would bring him a far greater income.

After we had breakfasted at home, I showed Walter Fewkes the prehistoric pottery and artifacts which I had collected from the many small ruins all about our post. In fact, our store building and our wool barn had been partly constructed with stones taken from walls and houses of the Anat-sazi (ancient people). Fewkes did not seem to be too much impressed with my collection. He said, "Why do you spend your time collecting these pots and stones? They have been safe in the earth for two thousand years and will last longer there than anywhere else. You are living now among a primitive people whose culture has been little affected by contact with white people. You have a golden opportunity to study and record their customs and their religion along with the symbolism."

This was a truth which I had already dimly perceived, and now it became a definite objective, his advice influencing many of my future endeavors.

13. "Flu" and a Ceremony

IN AUGUST OF 1918, I brought my baby, Lynette, home from the hospital in Gallup where I had remained three weeks after her birth to learn how to care for her. Klah came with his sister when he heard we were home, bringing his sacred medicine bundle and small bag of corn pollen to hold a Blessing Rite for her. It was a warm August day, and we carried the naked baby out into the sunshine to be sung over and sprinkled with sacred pollen. I was happy to have him take so much interest in our child, as from now on, he would be the only pediatrician or medical consultant I would have nearer than the government doctor stationed at Shiprock Agency. As he finished the rites, he presented her with an amulet of white shell and turquoise such as Navaho babies often wear tied to their hair or in the lobe of a pierced ear. I had been included in the ceremony, since I held the baby, and my forehead was marked with pollen which must remain for four days.

During that autumn and winter we saw little of Klah, although some of his family were in the store every day and we were kept informed of his trips, first to one side of the Reservation and then to another, to hold healing rites. Sometimes it was the short Wind Chant that was requested, or perhaps the five-day Hail Chant, but at least three times that fall he was called upon to hold the nine-day Yeibichai. Frequently he would ask Arthur to take him in our car if the distance was more than a few miles, for he had accumulated more and more articles that must accompany him. We now owned a small high-wheeled car called a Saxon-Six which would negotiate at least part of the ungraded trails.

For a year I did not have time to think of Navaho ceremonies, but the summer of 1919 found me again in attendance at the nearer gatherings. Arthur fixed straps to hold the baby-basket in the back seat of the car and, with one of Klah's grandnieces serving as baby-sitter to stay with Lynette while I spent the forenoon in the hogan watching the sand painting or the first part of the night witnessing the rites of exorcism, again I was memorizing symbols and ceremonies. It was not long until other medicine men were inviting me to attend the chants they held for the sick or for blessing of crops or homes. Gleason Begay and Hosteen Dijolie were Shooting Chant singers who lived in the lower valley and were much in demand. Although they invited me to see their sand paintings, they refused to allow them to be sketched on paper, and it was four years before I was finally given permission to record even one. They had waited to see whether or not some great disaster would befall Klah and when nothing did, they finally decided it would be all right to allow me to sketch a few of theirs.

At Klah's great ceremony another chanter had been initiated into the first step of his career as a Yeibichai medicine man. This young Navaho was Beaal Begay who had been helping Klah for some time and now decided to study to become an accepted chanter. He was well fitted for such a position as his father, Hosteen Beaal, was an Eagle Chanter—a ceremony in which eagles are caught to obtain their feathers for ritualistic purposes. It is also a healing rite to cure injuries by animals, scratches that have become infected, boils, and sores; also dizziness and fainting spells.

KLAH WITH ONE OF HIS YEIBICHAI TAPESTRIES

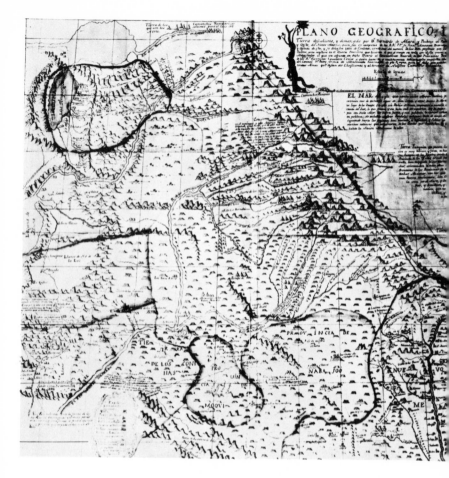

Escalante's map
showing the *"Provincia de Nabajoo"* (lower right)

Begay had memorized his father's ceremony and had accompanied the old man as long as he was able to hold these rites. The Eagle Chant ceremony was not considered a major rite and was now seldom used by the Navahos as it was easier to buy eagle feathers from the Jemez Indians than to pay for a five-day ceremony. Hosteen Beaal, although he had become crippled with arthritis and was almost blind, was highly respected and sometimes feared because he was a spiritualist medium who could pray himself into a trance and, while in that state, could review past scenes with startling accuracy. His mediumistic ability was much in demand for locating lost articles and lost horses and sheep and in tracing kidnaped children. He had demonstrated his ability so many times and with such amazing results that no one, Indian or white, questioned his unusual power. We had occasion to seek his help three times: once when our store was robbed of more than $3,000 worth of turquoise and silver jewelry that we were holding as pawn; once to locate a crazy Navaho who had tried to kill Mrs. Nelson, a neighboring trader's wife; and again when someone had opened the gate bars of our corral and made off with our three saddle horses.

This last was not much of a crime since the offenders had only "borrowed" the animals and expected to return them to the corral. Our horses were somewhat larger than most Navaho ponies, and a couple of Navaho boys had taken them to ride in the Shiprock races thinking to win a little easy money. Hosteen Beaal solved all three problems. For the first he took Arthur to a cave where the jewelry and most of the money was hidden; in the second case he traced the criminal to a mountain hideout; and for the third he

143

told us where we would find the horses. After this there was not much theft in our valley.

His son, Beaal Begay, did not possess any mediumistic powers, but he had a retentive memory, and during the years he traveled from ceremony to ceremony with Klah, he memorized every detail until he was able to conduct the whole chant. There were times when he would be the only medicine man in charge for the first four days, Klah arriving to preside during the last five. When he died of a kidney ailment, it was a great tragedy for Klah, who never attempted to teach another neophyte, and was sad to realize that when he was gone there would be no one to carry on his ceremony.

It was in the late fall of 1919 when Klah arrived at our post on his return from holding a ceremony in southern Colorado and a visit to the city of Durango. When he came into the store, Arthur realized at once that he was very ill and could hardly walk. He told him to sit down and gave him aspirin and water. I made hot coffee and asked if he wanted food, but he refused to eat. He was burning with fever and his eyes were bloodshot. This was the first case of the dreaded "flu" on our side of the Reservation. Arthur wanted Klah to go to bed in one of our tourist cabins where we could care for him, but he insisted that he must go to his own hogan where he had the herbs and powders to cure this illness. Arthur then took him to his home in the car, taking along a couple of cartons of food supplies. He wanted to notify Klah's sister and mother of his arrival, but Klah refused to permit this, saying, "I know this illness! It is the same that my great grandfather had when he was carried to Fort Wingate to sign the 'Bear Spring's Treaty,' and then it came again in my father's time and killed a great many people. If I move about, it will spread all over the Reservation and many will die." So Arthur built a fire in the fireplace and left him alone to struggle through the flu, and it was ten days before he came to the store again.

The disease did not spread at this time since he had maintained a strict quarantine, staying in his hogan, breathing herb fumigants, and drinking quantities of bitter (native quinine) tea, which finally effected a cure. Thus he was immunized and ready to care for his clan members when the influenza epidemic finally hit us.

Flu did not develop to alarming proportions around us until three months later, and then it was everywhere. During February, 1920, the weather was terrible, being mostly a series of wind-blown sleet storms turning to snow and ice. This month was known as "the hunger Moon" when food supplies were running low and many Navaho families were rationing their store of corn and beans to make them last until spring, and the sheep were much too thin to kill for mutton. There was always sickness at this time, but never like the present.

The first persons to die were buried in the accustomed manner, but soon death struck too fast and the living members of the family were too sick and too weak to attend to the burials. Throughout the valley there were many deserted hogans containing two or three corpses, wrapped in their blankets and covered with a little brush, loose earth, or ashes. The fleeing relatives did their best to block the doors and the smoke holes with logs and brush to prevent entry by coyotes and wild dogs. Small children and old people were the first victims, but the flu played no favorites and soon the death rate was just as high among the strong men and women. The whole atmosphere was filled with dread and nervous tension that no one could escape. The thought of death in every hogan, the angry rattle of sleet on our metal roof, the dark, stormy days, and the thin wailing "Yay-Yap-Yir-r-r" of the coyotes from every direction at night filled us with a sense of utter desolation.

It has been estimated that one-tenth of the entire Navaho population died that winter, and I believe that estimate is far too low. After the epidemic had passed its peak, the agent at Shiprock sent out teams of men to bury the corpses and burn the death hogans. Three of our household did not catch the flu at this time. My Navaho maid, Louise Bicenti, Lynette, and I were among the lucky few who seemed immune. When Arthur came down with the disease, I isolated him in the living room with the couch for his bed; then closing the doors that led to the bedroom and the kitchen, I calked the cracks with rags. Klah came and gave me some herbs to put on the coals of the fireplace to make a fumigant and also some powdered leaves to make a black tea. These, with aspirin and cod-liver oil, were all the medicines I had. Twice a day I changed my clothing and went around through the front door to take Arthur food and coal for his fire and to see that he was comfortable. Farmington, seventy-five miles to the north, and Gallup, sixty-five miles to the south, were quarantined, so there was no travel on the highway. Once I saw a car coming and ran out to hail it. The driver was a doctor who had been sent by the government to relieve the situation at the Shiprock Indian School forty-five miles north of us, where the hospital, the dormitories, and the recreation rooms were filled with cots to accommodate the sick children. This doctor refused to enter the house but did give me an additional supply of aspirin and a bottle of quinine tablets.

Hosteen Klah was busy taking care of the sick of his own clan and the families who lived nearby. As their hogans were clustered in groups, he did not have far to travel. He was the most successful doctor of any I heard about, losing only one member of his family, that being Mrs. Jim's baby, who was only six weeks old and who died of pneumonia. He saved the lives of two Navaho girls who came to his sister's hogan one night saying that their mother, father, and one brother were dead in their hogan and they had no place to go. It was a long time before the Navaho tribe recovered from the disastrous effects of this epidemic.

Shortly after the peak of the epidemic had passed, word was brought to Klah's sister that her eldest daughter, Ethnahbah, had been a flu victim. This daughter had lived with her husband and four children on the western side of the mountains. The messenger also reported that her husband was dead and there was no one to take care of the children. Upon receiving this sad news, Klah had one of the boys saddle a gentle horse, and, taking a roll of three or four blankets, he rode the sixty miles over the mountain. He found that the two older children were away at the government boarding school, but there was a small boy about three years old and a baby girl of five months left.

Making a carrying cradle of one blanket, he put the baby in it, put it across his shoulders and knotted the ends across his chest; then he folded another blanket on the saddle in front of him, making a seat for the boy. Two days later he came to the post to ask me for milk. We had a good cow

147

and I could give him all the milk he needed; also I found some bottles and nipples Lynette had used the year before which I took to his sister, explaining to her how they must be sterilized. Every day I took fresh milk and boiled the bottles, but my instructions were not understood, and the dust and flies were everywhere. This would never do. Some other way must be found to feed the baby.

I had heard the tale that when a Navaho mother died, her baby was smothered and placed in the same grave. I do not believe this was ever done, but the baby probably did die because of improper food. We carried canned milk in the store, and I decided to give Klah and his sister a supply of small cans with instructions that when the baby was hungry, one can was to be opened, the contents used immediately, and the can thrown away. This plan proved to be satisfactory, and two weeks later a nanny goat freshened and that was the perfect answer to the food problem. The nanny was kept in the corral and milked whenever the child was hungry.

Some time before this, Klah's two nieces had married brothers whose names were Sam and Jim Velieto, and we immediately gave the girls the names of "Mrs. Sam" and "Mrs. Jim," as these were easy to write in our books. These two young couples had homes of their own, and Klah and their grandmother had given them goodly flocks of sheep to start with. One day when Mrs. Sam was herding her flock toward the spring, she almost stepped on a rattlesnake, which uncoiled under her skirt and bit her on the ankle. Ordinarily the long, full skirts of the Navaho women are a protection from snake bites. But this time her foot had brushed the snake's coils and its head was only inches from her ankle. Klah came immediately and treated it by cutting the wound open and filling the cut with snake-bite medicine, the same root used by the Hopi medicine men who hold the snakes in their mouths during the Snake Dance. He then put some of the same medicine in goat's milk and had her drink all she could swallow. Mrs. Sam was a very sick girl, and the next day Arthur and Klah took her to Shiprock to be treated by the government doctor. He sterilized the wound and gave her some medicine, saying that her heart was all right and that Klah's treatment had probably saved her life. He asked for a piece of the root Klah had used, for he wished to have it analyzed to determine what medicinal properties it might contain.

Mrs. Sam recovered slowly, and after two weeks Klah decided to have a Snake Ceremony held for her. This was to be the Navaho Wind Chant, a five-day ceremony that deals with snakes, lightning, and cyclones, and for which a Wind Chanter would be needed. The nearest medicine man who knew this complete ceremony lived in Tees-nas-pas Canyon, sixteen miles to the north. His name was Tseh-yad-neejin (Black Rocks Piled Up), and he was almost blind, but he was still known as a powerful chanter.

Klah went to see him and satisfactory arrangements were made concerning time, place, and payment. One of the round stone hogans that was near the mountains was emptied of household articles, new adobe was tamped on the floor, and new blankets were hung over the door. Wood and water were placed handy, with bundles of herbs and tree branches on a high rack where they were out of reach of goats and horses. The old medicine man and his two helpers arrived a day early to make their preparations. There was a brush dressing room built somewhat to the south of the medicine lodge, to serve as a retreat for the patient and her women assistants. Near the dressing room was a temporary cookhouse.

The first day little took place except the blessing of the hogans, the medicine bundles, and all of the people who would take part in the ceremony, while the night chant was short and ended before midnight. A number of Klah's clan and of Sam's had assembled to assist with the sand paintings the next morning. When I entered the hogan, Klah was sitting near the door surrounded by the colored rocks, sand, and charcoal that he was grinding to make the dry paint for the sand symbols. Seven colors would be needed for this ceremony since all of the characters would wear brown masks and there must be pink to represent thunder. Because the grinding of sand, which is a part of Mother Earth, may well bring bad luck, an older relative of the patient assumes this task and then only after a blessing rite to ward away the evil consequences. There were pieces of bark to hold the piles of colored sands, and each painter was supplied with seven colors. Six men were working on the painting. The old chanter occupied the place of honor at the southwest with his pile of medicine bundles against the west wall, while his two assistants sat at the south. All three men had buffalo-hide lightning rattles. There were no Navaho women in the lodge and only men who were of her family. I gave the chanter a bright silk handkerchief for his head and the others packages of cigarettes; then, following Klah's direction, I sat on the floor at the northwest. The painting progressed rapidly with so many painters and soon showed four long figures of snake people standing on a four-colored cloud and carrying bows in their right hands with the arrows in the left. This central design was circled on three sides by a mirage (dotted colors) arc, while the eastern opening was guarded by two small figures of snakes. I was surprised to note that these snake figures wore blue masks such as belong to the Rainbow or Yei gods. The Snake people belong to the earth and therefore should wear brown masks.

When the sand-painted altar was completed, Tseh-yad-neejin sprinkled it with sacred pollen and Mrs. Sam was called. She came with her mother and two sisters, wearing new clothing, with her long black hair falling over her shoulders. The Wind Chanter led her to the place where she was to sit on the sand painting, then resumed his seat and took up his rattle, and the chant began. At various intervals he arose and performed parts of the ritual while his assistants carried on the chant. The last part of the healing was the burning of incense in front of the patient and of any member of the audience who desired it. Then the patient was helped to her feet and left the lodge accompanied by the other women. Now I was at liberty to ask about the masks. As the helpers scraped the loose sand from the adobe floor into blankets to be carried some distance to the north, I asked Tseh-yad-neejin why the faces of these Snake people had been blue. He replied that he had not been able to bring his brown masks with him and so had borrowed Klah's Yei masks, which were blue. The dancers in the night ceremony would wear the blue masks and so all the masks had to be blue.

I was late in arriving the next day, and when I saw Klah, I knew he was greatly disturbed about something. When

I examined the sand painting, I knew the reason. It was a circular design with the Snake people marching around a black central mountain. Some of these Snake figures were moving sunwise around the circle, but others were definitely headed in the opposite direction. Whether this had happened because of the chanter's poor eyesight or because the painters had been careless, I do not know. Klah had called the medicine man's attention to this error, but he refused to have the figures changed as he was afraid it would offend the snake spirits. So the sand painting was completed and the healing ritual performed while Klah's face plainly expressed disapproval of the whole proceeding. As soon as the women had left the lodge, he hurried after them, taking his pollen medicine bag to hold a Blessing Rite over Mrs. Sam in order to avert any evil consequences. This was the first time I had ever seen Klah angry at another medicine man, and it also was the first and last time I ever saw a sand painting that was not perfect used for a healing ceremony or for any other purpose.

There were two more days of sand paintings and then the body painting on the last night. Mrs. Sam's chest and back were painted with designs of the sun, the moon, and the four colors of wind trails. Her face was striped with white on her forehead, black below that, then blue from ear to ear, and a yellow bar across her chin. These markings would remain for four days before they could be washed off. With the coming of dawn, the fires were allowed to die, and the ceremony ended.

Not long after this we went to Gallup to select the trade goods we would have freighted out to us while the roads were in fair condition. For four or five months at a time during the winter and spring heavily loaded wagons could not be hauled over the mountains or through the muddy valleys. We had learned to have our supplies freighted to us during the dry seasons.

We secured our hotel accommodations, enjoyed a chef-cooked dinner, and attended a movie, a rare occurrence in our lives, and then retired for the night. The next morning I awoke with a high fever, too ill to be out of bed. Arthur took Lynette down to the dining room, where a waitress fed her cereal and milk, and then he called a doctor, who took one look at me and said I had the flu. St. Mary's Hospital was filled to overflowing, and there was nothing we could do but stay where we were. I believe someone who had occupied that room had had flu and the pillows and blankets had not been sterilized. Lynette came down with it the next day. Arthur hired a nurse, had another bed put in my room, and took an adjoining room for himself. We were there ten days.

When we finally arrived home, Klah came to talk to Arthur. He was very worried because I had been so ill and said it was because I had witnessed so many sand paintings and had been present when too many powerful prayers were recited. No one should do this until some ceremony had been held for him. We asked what ceremony he wished to hold, and he answered, "Five days of the Yeibichai." But this I flatly refused to endure. On four mornings during this ceremony the patient must take an emetic, and I was so constructed that an emetic made me deathly ill. It was good therapy for a Navaho, and I could see why any woman would be cured and never again admit that she was ill; but I was not a Navaho, and this ceremony was not for

153

me. He then suggested the three-day Apache Wind Chant, but this, too, had emetics, with the added discomfort of face blackening and body painting. I told him, "No! I would rather have whatever illness might come than to have it prevented in such an unpleasant manner." He was insistent that there must be a ceremony of some kind, and finally suggested the Hozhonji, or Blessing Chant. It lasted only two nights and was mostly a series of chanted prayers, punctuated by pollen sprinkling and the drinking of little sips of herb infusion. In the forenoon there would be the emergence sand painting and the pollen trail. It was really a beautiful ceremony, but one not to be entered into as a lark. For one thing, I would be required to remain awake both nights from sunset until dawn and the day between; and for another, I would be expected to memorize a prayer that took at least three-quarters of an hour to recite in duo with the medicine man.

My command of the Navaho language was not extensive, and these ancient prayer recitals contained archaic words that were not in use at the present time, their meaning all but lost. Arthur heartlessly remarked, "Oh, go ahead! Be a good sport! Klah will be hurt if you refuse!" So I agreed, and had Klah recite the prayer slowly so that I could write it down a week beforehand and do the best I could to commit it to memory. I had already learned to sit for hours at a time, with my feet folded under me, but all night in that position would not be so pleasant, and two nights would probably leave me paralyzed.

On the eve of the first night I went to the women's hogan where Klah's sister washed my hair and my necklace of white shells in yucca suds, after which the women accompanied me to the ceremonial lodge where Arthur and Klah were enjoying a friendly cigarette. There was a pollen design where I was to sit, with a few rainbow arcs around it. The only persons in the hogan were Klah's sister and two of her daughters, Klah, Arthur, and myself, this being strictly a family affair. The chant began, and my only trouble seemed to be in staying awake, for the monotonous rhythm made me sleepy. Then I found that I was not to sit all night in one position as Klah halted the chant to lay down a line of pollen to the south and I followed it to receive a pollen blessing from that direction, then went back to the center. Some time later this was repeated to the west, then to the north, and finally to the east; and when this eastern blessing ended, the ceremony was over. It was after five when Arthur and I went home.

About four hours later we were called back to the ceremonial hogan as the painting had been completed. This could hardly be termed a "sand painting," although it was laid out in colors in the same manner. For this one, however, no sand had been used. The background was a rectangle with a smaller square on top, made of white corn meal. The blue stalk of corn, which extended from bottom to top, was of blue corn meal outlined in yellow pollen. The two figures standing below the corn were of white corn meal outlined with red from flower petals, the blue bird was made with blue pollen, and the black was charcoal with no sand. The two white figures represented the Spirit Givers and the white rectangle the house of life. The corn with its four bars and four pollen footprints was the ladder of life through its four stages, and above it was the blue bird indicating peace and happiness as a final goal.

It was a beautiful way of reminding a participant that only by personal effort in mounting the ladder of life can spiritual strength be acquired and the ending be peace and happiness. After a period of chanting, Klah started on the Pollen Trail and I followed in his footsteps. His sister and the girls came behind me, and I believe Arthur was the last in line. Klah recited the prayer as he went, a long stanza at every step, and I echoed his words, doing my best to remember how it went. When we finally emerged from the spirit's house, I was given a sip of herb infusion and the remainder was sprinkled over my head. That night the ceremony of the previous night was repeated, and so my "ceremony" was completed.

Word of this ceremony held over a white woman gradually spread over most of the Navaho Reservation, and I believe that from that time on I was regarded as a member of the Navaho tribe. Whenever I desired to witness a sand painting or a healing rite on any part of the Reservation, even among Indians I had never seen before, all I needed to say to gain entrance was, "I have had a ceremony."

14. Ceremonial Rugs and a Crown Prince

URING 1919 and 1920 the Reservation was very quiet as the Dinnae sought to recover from their great disaster. There were few large ceremonies and no social gatherings of any other nature. One day as Klah was helping me with my sand-painting collection, I asked why he did not weave a rug with a ceremonial design. He said that the sacred symbols should not be put into a rug that would be placed on the floor and walked on day after day. I assured him that a blanket of this type would never be used on the floor but would be hung on the wall of some museum. He said he would think about it.

After talking it over with his family, he decided it would be all right to weave the first large sand painting of the Yeibichai, which is called "The Whirling Log Painting." The women of his family all had looms for weaving ordinary rugs, but they were not large enough for Klah. He had logs brought from the mountain and built a loom that would hold a rug twelve feet square. Then came the problem of finding the right wool. Klah insisted that the rug have a background of native tan wool that was not dyed. A rug of this size would require twenty pounds of raw wool, and as this tan color was found only on the underside of the brown sheep, it did not seem possible to collect this much. Arthur and Klah motored to every trading post on our side of the Reservation, buying a few pounds of tan wool at each until they had the right amount.

We sent to Juárez for indigo and cochineal dyes, and

Klah's sister made a bright yellow from goldenrod; the other colors were the natural wool colors. Grandma Klah started spinning, and soon a box of large balls of finely spun yarn was ready for Klah's use. The loom was erected on the south side of Klah's hogan, and we supplied the canvas with which to cover it when he was not working. Many of the other Navahos in our valley were critical of this project as they thought the making of an accurate sand painting in permanent form would bring disaster to the entire tribe. But Klah was too powerful in medicine-man status for them to say anything to him, so they voiced their complaints to Arthur, who became really worried for fear some fanatic would slash the rug and destroy the loom before the work could be completed. He hired a man to stay with Klah and guard the loom at night, but Klah was never worried. He chanted his prayers and said that nothing would happen—nothing did!

While this Whirling Log was still on the loom, Mr. and Mrs. King C. Gillette and a group of friends crossed the Reservation on their way to visit the prehistoric ruins at Mesa Verde. When they stopped at our post to have lunch, we found that Mrs. Gillette was quite interested in rare Navaho rugs. Arthur took them to Klah's hogan to see the ceremonial tapestry he was weaving, and she decided at once to buy it when it was completed. Arthur was glad to arrange a sale, but asked to keep the rug until after the Navaho Ceremonial in Gallup in September. Here it was displayed and won the blue ribbon for rugs of its class. Then it was sent to Palm Springs to Mrs. Gillette, who was so pleased with it that she wrote and asked if we could have Klah weave two more rugs to complete the set of Yeibichai

Left to right: Klah, Arthur Newcomb, Mary Cabot Wheelwright, and
Clyde Beaal at Northeast Harbor, Maine

KLAH IN GALLUP
on his way to Chicago in 1934

paintings she had seen in a ceremony in Arizona. We were glad to receive her order, and Klah again began preparing wool for weaving. Now he was definitely started on a new vocation—that of weaver of ceremonial rugs.

Before her order arrived, Klah had strung warp on his loom and was at work on another tapestry, this time a Hail Chant painting, which he completed in the summer of 1921, and we were permitted to exhibit it at the Gallup Ceremonial that fall. While on display it was purchased by Mary Cabot Wheelwright of Boston, who was a visitor at the Gallup Fair.

A week after the Fair, we received an inquiry from the San Gabriel Dude Ranch asking if we could furnish accommodations for a party of three who were crossing the Reservation on horseback and would like a place to stay for a couple of nights, and also if we could supply grain for four horses for the remainder of the trip to the Canyon de Chelly. Arthur replied that we would be glad to have them with us and that we would be able to furnish hay and grain. One afternoon a week or so later, these guests arrived. They were Mary Wheelwright, Evelyn Sears, and their guide, Orville Cox. They had come from Alcalde by way of Jemez Pass and had been in the saddle five days. Although a pack horse carried comfortable camping equipment, they were glad to come into the house and have real beds and home-cooked food.

The first evening we asked Klah to dine with us and then amuse our guests by telling Navaho legends. I imagine that this was the first time either of these eastern women had sat at the same table with a Navaho Indian, but both carried through with graciousness. The stories Klah told

159

that evening were a mixture of folk tale and myth that were amusing but had no religious significance. Klah was quite pleased when Mary mentioned this fact. Before he left, she asked if he would tell her something of his religion if she should return. He thought for a while and then answered, "Yes, if you really wish to know." She returned to Newcomb many times.

Since the horses had been five days with short rations and needed a rest, the party decided to stay a couple of days to allow them to get into shape again. Klah had gone to a Navaho home across the Río Chaco about forty miles to the east of our post to hold a three-day Wind Chant. Arthur asked our three guests if they would like to visit the lodge and see something of the ceremony. He did not think to tell them that there was only a trail leading to this place and that these trails were never meant for cars. I was not too sure they would be able to cross the three unbridged arroyos, but with three men in the car they should be able to push it out of difficulties. I prepared two boxes of food and three Thermos jugs of water, then gave them several blankets. Arthur took an extra five-gallon can of gasoline, remarking, "You never can tell."

The Río Chaco is an intermittent stream, sometimes carrying as much as five feet of water; at other times it is just a river of bottomless sand. At this time of year there was no water, and the Indians had built a wagon road from bank to bank by covering the sand with rabbit brush, so it looked passable. Before the car reached the river, a hard-gusty sandstorm hit them, and they halted to fasten the curtains and then drove down the bank and started across the dry river bed. Some of the brush had blown away, but they kept going until they had almost reached the opposite bank, where the brush was completely gone and the sand was piled in drifts. The more the wheels spun, the deeper the car sank into the sand.

Everyone realized they were hopelessly stopped, but since they could see the ceremonial hogan on the higher ground, they decided to walk the rest of the way, each one carrying a blanket and a parcel of food. The men carried the Thermos jugs. The wind was fierce and nearly tore the blankets from their arms, but they reached the lodge, which was a small six-sided hogan with a blanket over the door. As they entered, they saw that it contained about twenty-five Navahos, both men and women, and that the patient was a young girl. It did not seem that there would be room for five more persons, but the Indians vacated a place on the north side where they could sit on their folded blankets. They stayed until the rites ended about midnight, and then did not know what to do. The sandstorm still swept across the desert, and the car was almost completely buried.

There was a trading post not far away owned by a bachelor whom we called Shorty, and this was the only shelter for miles around. They went to the post and asked to spend the remainder of the night. There were four rooms and twenty people, but at least they were out of the wind. The two women were given some extra blankets and quartered in the rug room, where they spent a most uncomfortable night, so that they were very glad indeed when day arrived. Many men joined in helping shovel the sand away from the car and filling the hole with brush. When the car was started and turned around, they went ahead to mend the broken places in the road, and the journey back to our post was made without trouble. This was Mary Wheelwright's first ceremony in Navaho country, but it was not the last, as she returned to witness many more, but Miss Sears never came back.

More and more orders were received for ceremonial tapestries, and although Klah wove steadily in his spare time, he could not fill them all. He decided to hold the full nine-day Yeibichai ceremony over his two nieces, invoking the protection of the immortals for their future activities. Then he gave his twelve by twelve loom to Mrs. Sam and had another of the same size built for Mrs. Jim. For himself he procured longer poles and erected a loom that would hold a rug fifteen by fifteen feet, but he generally strung his warp so that the rug would be twelve by thirteen feet. While the girls were weaving, he watched them day by day to be sure there were no mistakes to offend the gods, and when the rugs were finished, he sang the Hozhonie prayers over the girls to banish all evil influences. But even with all of this ceremonial protection, there were older Navahos who expected the girls to be afflicted with blindness because of gazing too long at the sacred symbols or perhaps to become paralyzed in their arms for weaving these symbols into a rug. After a few years had passed and neither Klah or the girls had suffered ill effects, many weavers decided to make "figure blankets," which were beautiful and brought high prices, but no one else dared make an exact copy of a ceremonial sand painting. As a result, those woven by Klah and his nieces remained unique in the field of Navaho handwoven tapestries.

The next year oil was discovered at Table Mesa and a pipe line was laid from the wells to the railroad shipping point at Gallup. This did not affect us or the Indians in any way except by bettering the roads. The oil company furnished the basic material and the government black-topped a narrow strip of road from Gallup to Shiprock which looked like a black ribbon running on and on forever with never a crossing. It was a great improvement to have a road that did not blow away during the season of sandstorms. The oil company also ran a telephone line beside the road and permitted us to attach a phone. Thus gradually our pioneer life acquired a few modern conveniences, but our water supply was always inadequate. The water which came from our pump was so impregnated with minerals that one chemist who tested it termed it "mineral soup." We hauled our drinking and cooking water from a warm spring five miles away, the best water on the Reservation.

In October of 1923, Lynette and I went to stay with my sister and family in Colorado. On November 27, Thanksgiving Day, my second baby girl was born and was named Priscilla, for my mother. We remained in Colorado, where Arthur joined us for the Christmas festivities, then we took the train to Gallup with the baby in a large market basket, arriving at the post on New Year's Day. Klah came to hold the Blessing Ceremony, this time in front of our huge fireplace as the weather had turned bitterly cold, the wind piling drifts of snow and sleet four feet high in some places. The storms continued throughout January and February with no moderation of the temperature. This was disastrous for the Navaho sheepowners as they depended on open grazing for their flocks the year round. Hosteen Bichai, the wealthiest sheepowner in our valley, lost more than half of his flock, and remarked when he came to the store, "I was a rich man once, I am a poor man now." Klah and his family did not lose as many as most, probably because they stayed right with their sheep and, when a weak one went down, would carry it to an empty hogan and feed it shelled corn. At one time they had four hogans filled with the sheep they were hand-feeding, and when their store of corn was gone, Klah bought nearly all of the corn we had in our grain room. The next spring the grass on the mesa was knee high, but there were few sheep left to eat it.

And so the years passed rapidly, some lean and others bountiful. Every fall Klah and his nieces had new sand-painting tapestries for us to exhibit at the Gallup Ceremonial, and these continued to take prizes as the most exceptional of all Navaho weaving. During the years between 1919 and the time of his death in 1937, Klah wove twenty-five sand-painting tapestries and his nieces wove almost as many more. Mary Wheelwright bought twelve that were woven by Klah and nine that were made by the nieces. These are now on display in the Museum of Navajo Ceremonial Arts at Santa Fe, New Mexico. Mrs. King C. Gillette bought four, two of which are in the Read Mullen Museum at Phoenix, Mrs. Harold Gladwin took three of Klah's and two made by his nieces, all five of which may be seen in the Arizona State Museum in Flagstaff. Mrs. E. O. Barnes owns one which she has placed in the Santa Fe Museum. I still own Klah's last large tapestry, which was not quite finished at the time of his death. I also have one from each of the nieces. We made photographs and kept complete records of all the ceremonial rugs made by these three weavers, but they were lost in the fire which destroyed our trading post in 1936.

During April and May of 1926, the newspapers were headlining the visit of the Crown Prince of Sweden and his wife, the Princess Louise, who were then touring the United States. One of the places he was eager to visit was the Mesa Verde National Park with its prehistoric ruins. Years before, his father, the King of Sweden, had purchased a large collection of prehistoric relics that had been taken from these ruins, which now were on display in the Royal Museum of Stockholm. He wished to see the ancient houses where these things had been found.

We watched the news items to be sure of the time he would be crossing the Navaho Reservation and we read about Henry Ford's shipping six specially built Lincoln cars to Gallup for their use. The Santa Fe Railroad brought the royal party to Gallup in a private car, and from there they drove north in the Lincolns. On their way to the park they did not pass our post but followed a road nearer the mountains in order to pause for lunch at the Toadlena Government Indian School. Ten days later a car carrying newspaper reporters from every large city in the United States stopped at the post taking time to deliver a message that the Crown Prince and his party would be at our place for lunch. Then the car drove rapidly away as all were in a hurry to reach the nearest telegraph office.

It was Tuesday and washday at the Newcomb trading post. There was a large copper boiler on the kitchen range and my two maids were busy with tubs and washboards on the back porch, while two boys brought water from the arroyo. All this—and only two hours to prepare lunch for twenty members of royalty! Well, it can be done, but it was hard on my spring crop of young fryers. By one o'clock fifteen young chickens were fried and ready for the last browning, potatoes were creamed, canned vegetables were ready, fruit salad also from cans, and baking powder biscuits ready for the oven. For dessert, there was a large spice cake to be served with whipped cream. Then we proceeded to fill all available pitchers and water bottles with cold drinks —iced tea, lemonade, coffee, and ice water, as the day was unusually warm. Our front porch was fourteen feet long by eight wide, and this we carpeted with Navaho rugs and erected plank tables down the center to be covered with my best white table linen.

Finally the guests arrived, and my two Navaho girls and I served the plates. We started pouring the iced drinks, but these were not wanted. Nearly everyone asked for hot tea, and, much to my embarrassment, we had no hot water. While they were eating, Arthur sent a boy to ask Klah to come and meet the Prince and his party. The men were in the store examining jewelry and trinkets when he arrived. He looked at the group and immediately walked to the Prince to shake hands. How he knew which man was the Prince is odd, for while many of the other men wore their insignia, the Prince was dressed as any other tourist might have been. Klah welcomed the Prince to Navaho country, and then shook hands with other members of the royal party. The Prince asked, "Is this the chief or king?" and Arthur said, "No, the Navahos have no king, but he is an important medicine man." The Prince remarked, "He has the dignity of royalty." The Prince carried a camera and asked if he might take Klah's picture. Given an assent, he took a number in several different poses. Then he asked what kind of pet animal was sitting on Lynette's shoulder and was told that it was a tame prairie dog. He was much amused when the little animal scrambled up her long curls to sit on top of her head and barked at anyone who came near. He took more pictures of Lynette and her pet, and I hoped he would send us copies, but none ever came.

In the winter of 1927, Mary Wheelwright decided to make recordings of the hundreds of chants Klah used in his Yeibichai ceremony. Lynette was boarding in Farmington and Priscilla was four years old. Mary had a recorder sent to her home in Alcalde and engaged Professor Herzog to write the music and Mr. Harry Hoijer to write the translations of the songs. Arthur, Klah, Clyde, Priscilla, and I went to Alcalde to stay for two months. Mr. and Mrs. Albert Staples were caring for the place in Mary's absence, and Mrs. Staples, with the help of two Mexican girls, undertook the task of seeing that we were fed. In order that my time might not be wasted, Mary hired Mrs. Stevenson as typist to write down the descriptions of one hundred or more sand paintings that belonged to Klah's different chants as I related them verbally. Working hours were not long or continuous because Klah's voice grew husky after two or three hours of chanting and did not record clearly. Mrs. Stevenson had brought her daughter, Dorothy, who was about Priscilla's age, and the two small girls amused themselves in the patio by crawling through the chimney of the outdoor oven, causing everyone to marvel at how they could get themselves so dirty.

The weather for the most part was beautiful, and February seemed like spring. Mr. and Mrs. Staples had visited the fiestas at the Indian pueblos many times and had become acquainted with many of the governors and important families, even as far away as Taos. They kept a schedule of winter ceremonies, and when a dance date appeared on the calendar, we would take a day off, Tina Staples would pack a large basket of lunch, and "Staples" would drive us to the pueblo where the fiesta was taking place. This was our first contact with winter festivities among the Puebloans, and we found it very interesting. Klah was especially pleased to witness these rites, as he understood them much better than we did. Mr. Staples took extra pains to have Klah meet the governors and the medicine men of each pueblo and took him into their homes while we were buying trinkets and souvenirs. These two months were a pleasant interlude in a winter of ordinary trading.

The next spring we received word that stockmen would visit the Reservation with government orders to kill all surplus horses, goats, and sheep. As the Navahos did not own much cattle, cattle were not included in the reduction lists. A census of all livestock owned by each Navaho family would be taken and then they would be told how many sheep, goats, and horses they could keep on a "minimum existence" basis. The rest were to be brought to a designated place to be slaughtered. The government paid a small amount for each animal destroyed. The horses, at four dollars a head, were driven to fox farms and glue factories, while the sheep and goats were killed on the spot, the owners receiving two dollars for each. Once again the Navahos were reduced to semistarvation. Klah did not like to lose his horses, but he now owned no goats and few sheep, for he had divided his flock with many relatives in order to devote his time to ceremonies.

Discouragement was general across the Reservation,

and again a pilgrimage was arranged to the Page of Prophecy at the Shining Sands. Five medicine men were to go this time, and the one from our valley was Hosteen Dijoli. We gave him a small prehistoric pottery bowl and lent him a large buckskin that still had its hair. They followed the same trail as the previous group and camped at the same places, sang the same prayers, and looked at the same Page. We were glad when they returned to hear that their report was favorable and indicated good crops, heavy rains, and an increase in population. Two wide tracks across the sand were interpreted later to indicate the coming of the automobile for Navaho use in marketing their sheep and wool.

After the lambs were sold in the fall, we decided to spend the winter in Phoenix in order to put the girls in a good school and also to enjoy a warmer climate. Lynette was now in the sixth grade and Priscilla would be entering the first. We rented a furnished house and moved to Phoenix in September, taking Lucy Hapaha with us. Arthur commuted between the two places. In October, Mary decided to come to Phoenix and have Arthur bring Klah and Clyde so that she could obtain the myth and an account of the rites of the Hail Chant. We found tourist cabins for the two men not far from us, and Mary took a suite at the Westward Ho. As the weather was quite warm, most of the recording was done on our large front porch, which boasted comfortable chairs and a swing. Klah told the legend and Clyde interpreted, while Mary and Arthur alternated in writing it down. The two girls were in school, and Lucy and I served meals and saw that everything ran smoothly. On Saturdays we visited the Roosevelt Dam, the Pima and the Papago Indian reserves, and many other scenic places before Arthur took the two Navahos back to the Reservation and Mary went to New York for the opera season.

At Christmas time the girls were given two and one-half weeks' vacation, and we went back to the post. Christmas at our Reservation trading post was one of the great events of the year. Two or three days before the real Christmas Day arrived, we bought a young beef for the Navahos to barbecue. They dug the fire pit, brought the wood, and started the roasting process a day ahead of the feast, and someone stayed near to keep the fires at an even level all night. The next day we furnished the other items that made up the menu. First, there were two or three large cartons of bakery bread which they considered a treat as they generally baked their own. Then there were a couple of galvanized tubs filled with baked beans mixed with chili peppers and a large dishpan overflowing with sliced onions. A wash boiler was used to make the coffee, and it had to be refilled two or three times. Frosted cookies completed the menu.

This was the Christmas dinner, but the part the Navahos really thought of as "Kishmus" was the sack of treats each Navaho man, woman, and child received after the feast was over. A week beforehand we had invited Klah and his family to the post to help in filling the paper sacks. We had estimated our needs for this occasion and had our freighters bring extra supplies, and with these we filled at least 250 sacks for our holiday guests. There were many more than our usual customers, for Navaho families came from far and wide to share the food and the treats. We tried to serve our neighbors first as sometimes the sacks did not go all the way around. But when that happened, we had bins of winter apples we could substitute.

A sample sack was filled and placed on the counter. It contained one apple, one orange, a double handful of peanuts, a couple of cookies, a package of gum, and a small sack of mixed candies. It took more than two days to fill the "Kishmus" sacks, but we all ate peanuts and apples, drank red pop, and had a wonderful time.

We were not the only traders who held a "Kishmus" for the Navahos, and the school at Toadlena generally served a mutton dinner to all the parents of the school children, generally the day after our barbecue. As soon as our guests had received their sacks, we would see them hurrying to their horses or wagons to be on their way to the next place on their lists. Some of them were able, by good timing and moving about at night, to participate in three or four feasts with either gifts or sacks of treats.

The last months of our stay in Phoenix were quite harrowing. It rained until it became evident that our house was built over an old lake bed. The graveled surface of the driveway broke through, disclosing fluid black mud beneath, and my car sank in the quag until it covered the floor. The gutters ran with rivers of water, and it was impossible for the girls to walk to school. The rains did not last long, however, and when they ended, I hired a wrecker with a derrick to drag my car to dry land. But when scarlet fever signs were placed on the front doors of the two houses nearest us, I telephoned Arthur to come and take us back to the Reservation. It was just possible that we might pay too high a price for a little education. We returned to the post the last day of March, 1929.

15. An Eastern Vacation

MANY OF MARY'S FRIENDS and relatives had wondered why she spent so much of her time and money on the Navaho Reservation. They did not see how she could be so much interested in a medicine man and his primitive religion. Since she could not bring them all to the Navaho country to meet Klah, she decided to take Klah to her summer home in Maine to meet them. Her summer home was on the Atlantic Coast at Northeast Harbor, and here she made preparations to entertain Hosteen Klah as guest of honor, Clyde Beaal as interpreter, and Arthur and myself as co-ordinators. Her boathouse in the cove had an upper deck, which she converted into a sitting room and a bedroom to accommodate the two Navahos. Arthur and I were house guests.

When we first heard about this proposed trip, we did not think it would be possible. First, we had no one to handle our Indian trade while we were away; second, the girls were not included in the invitation and we had no place to leave them while we were gone; and third, Klah and Clyde had other plans for the summer. But one by one these difficulties were overcome. A young Indian trader by the name of Walter Wells came to work for us. A cousin in Wisconsin offered to care for the girls at her summer cottage at Springbank if we would bring them to her. And when the Indians learned that all of their expenses were to be paid, they were eager to go.

Buick cars that year were large and roomy, with deep trunks at the back, but even so, Arthur bought a baggage carrier for the top and I sent the girls' trunk to Wisconsin by express. It was a bit crowded with six in the car the first half of the journey, but we had no difficulty in finding accommodations along the way. At two tourist courts we were labled "Oklahoma Indians who have struck oil."

We found things quite different when we were east of the Missouri River; here the hotels, courts, and lodging houses maintained a strict color bar and we could find no place to stay. The last night before we reached the summer resort in Wisconsin, Arthur drove all night. At Springbank we had engaged two cabins for a short rest and to see the girls settled for the month we would be in the East. I had several aunts and uncles living on farms in this part of Wisconsin who were all interested in meeting our Navaho friends and invited them to sumptuous meals of roast beef and strawberries with thick cream. I had advised them not to serve chicken or turkey, for the two Navahos would not have eaten either one. The taboo against eating the flesh of anything that has feathers is still obeyed. Klah was happy to meet my relatives and called my Aunt Anna "Nu-mah" (your mother) from then on. The cousin who had offered to care for Lynette and Priscilla was also their godmother and was pleased to have them with her.

From Wisconsin to Northeast Harbor the car was not so crowded, but we had other troubles. We found that all the remainder of the journey we were classed as "colored" and could enter very few dining places and no hotels whatever. If we stopped in towns to allow Klah or Clyde a chance to buy cigarettes or cold drinks, pedestrians stopped to gaze and crowds formed around them while someone was sure to ask, "Are these real Indians?" Some even inquired if we were a "medicine show." At first we found it amusing and did not mind, but when night came and we were barred from several cafés and could find no hotel accommodations, it ceased to be a joke. It was eleven o'clock when a clerk at a Green Gables tourist court finally rented us a couple of rooms for the night, and this may have been because he was too sleepy to notice who was with us.

While Arthur was buying the gas, I visited a grocery where I bought everything I thought we might need for the day's meals, and it was a good thing I did. At noon we stopped in a small town and entered a café. Before we were seated, there was a crowd around the car in front of the open café door. Children were afraid to come close and even the grownups remained at a discreet distance. The waitresses were too much surprised even to come and take our orders. I sincerely wished that Clyde could have been carrying a tomahawk and had waved it around his head while emitting an outlandish war whoop. Those people would have had something to tell their children and grand-children about nearly being scalped by wild Indians. We never did get served, but climbed back into the car, drove out of town, and lunched on the food I had purchased. Not only was all of this annoying, but it used up precious time and caused us to be a day behind the schedule we had planned and shortened our stay.

One afternoon we decided to look for lodgings early, since there were few tourist courts along our route. However, occasionally there were beautiful white farmhouses with signs on the lawns which read, "Rooms for Tourists." It was about half-past five when we came to one of these signs and decided to ask for accommodations. Arthur stopped the car in front of the fence and I opened the gate and walked up the path. In answer to my knock, a prim, middle-aged woman came to unlock the screen and ask me inside. I did not go in, but stepped back on the path and said, "We are four tourists who would like to engage rooms for one night, I am wondering if you object to taking Indians." She looked me over slowly and then looked at Arthur who was removing the radiator cap. She took her time before answering and I could almost hear her thoughts. "Well, these may be Indians but they do not look much different from ordinary tourists."

Then she said, "No, I do not object to Indians. I have two nice rooms upstairs, and there is a bathroom on the same floor."

Again I said, "Are you sure you have no objections to Indians?"

She smiled as she answered, "Oh, certainly not. No objection whatever."

"I will tell the others," I said, and nodded my head at Arthur as I walked toward the car. At this signal, Klah and Clyde stepped from the car and draped their brightly colored blankets over their arms. They had taken a few steps toward the house when I heard a little shriek and turned to look at the woman. She had rushed onto the porch, slammed and hooked the screen door, and was saying over and over, "No! Oh, no! No!"

I smiled at her, for I had expected somethink like this to happen. "You mean that you have changed your mind?" I asked.

"Yes, Oh yes!" she stammered. "My husband will be home any time now and he would not like it."

I doubted the existence of a husband, but walked to the car, remarking as I climbed in, "No luck there."

About an hour later, we stopped at another large white farmhouse with a "Rooms for Rent" sign on the lawn. We might be turned away, but it would do no harm to ask. A man came to answer my knock at the door. When I asked my usual question about securing rooms for Indians, he seemed quite excited and called his wife. She, too, was interested, and both walked to the car with me. When they saw Klah and Clyde, their eyes fairly glistened. The wife said, "What a chance for the boys to know some real Indians." The man showed us where to park the car and, taking my suitcase, led the way into the house. The family were all there to welcome us—three big boys, two smaller girls, and a hired man who evidently was treated as one of the family. They had finished their evening meal, but all hands joined in resetting the table while the mother warmed up platters of meat and bowls of mashed potatoes with thick brown gravy. There was homemade bread and blackberry pie. I think food had never tasted quite so good. I was tired and went immediately to my room, but the men sat on the porch and answered questions late into the night. The friendliness of this family did much to make us forget the snubs we had received at other places.

We drove into Cleveland the next day and inquired our way to the home of some friends who had spent a couple of days at our post. They were Mr. and Mrs. J. Forbes, and they had invited us to stay the night with them. Klah and Clyde had rooms above the garage which suited them better than being in the house, as they felt free to do a little sight-seeing. That evening we were to dine at the Lake Shore Country Club, so I donned my Navaho squaw dress, which had a very full dark-green sateen skirt with a bright yellow velveteen blouse and much turquoise and silver jewelry. My hair was dark brown, and I combed it straight back and tied it in a knot at the back of my head. I think that many who saw me believe to this day that I was a Navaho. There were no color restrictions in the dining room, but we were placed in an alcove near enough to see and be seen. After dinner, Klah chanted to the rhythm of Clyde's basket drum. The songs he sang were not ceremonial but the short folk songs such as "The Bluebird Song," "The Owl Song," "The Dawn Song," and "The Chattering Squirrel." Clyde interpreted as each ended.

In the morning, Mr. Forbes took Arthur to the docks to buy boat tickets to Buffalo and to check our car into the ship's hold. The steamer left at noon, with the four of us standing on deck waving good-bye to Mrs. Forbes and her two daughters. The Indians were thrilled with their first boat ride, and I was sorry when the fog turned into a misty rain that obscured our view in every direction. I asked Klah what the songs he sang the night before had been taken from. When he answered, "From the Rain Ceremony," I said, "That does it! Our good weather is over; now it will rain forever!" The next morning we took the car off the boat at Buffalo, the rain was pouring down with a monotony that promised much more of the same. All across the state of

New York the roads gleamed wetly, and water splashed from every dip. Clyde remarked that this would be fine for New Mexico, but seemed wasted here.

In Boston, other friends who had visited us on the Reservation had reserved rooms for us at one of the larger hotels. When we presented our reservations at the desk, the clerk, the doorman, the bellboys, in fact the whole staff nearly fainted. But the name on our card was that of the hotel's largest stockholder, so accommodations were arranged. We were given quite a suite on the fourth floor and told that our meals would be served in our rooms with no extra charge, and please do not use the lounges or the foyer. They seemed greatly relieved when we said we were leaving early the next morning.

The next afternoon we arrived at Mary's home in Northeast Harbor. The house stood on a point of land overlooking the bay and a sandy cove where the boathouse was located. The deck of the boathouse consisted of two rooms which were now furnished for Klah and Clyde. On the other side of the house, the terrain rose steep and rocky, with pines, spruce, and wild vegetation in its native forms. A good automobile road climbed up this side, passed under a portico, and then to a three-car garage. On the next point of land stood the Atwater summer home, and beyond that, the home of the Edsel Fords. On the other side, but too far away to be seen, was the summer estate of John D. Rockefeller, Jr., and beyond that, the homes of many other eastern millionaires.

We had been a week on the road, and it would take us almost as long to return. Since we had planned to be gone a month, that limited our stay at Northeast Harbor to two weeks. Mary had plans for every hour of those fourteen days. The second day she asked Klah to make a sand painting on the flagged terrace east of the house. I thought the sand along the shore would be all right, but Klah said it would not, as it was filled with bits of crushed shell that would cut his fingers, so we motored back into the hills until we found a ledge of white sandstone, and beneath it quantities of soft, white sand. There were no other native sand colors except brown, so we bought diamond dyes to mix with the white sand to make red, yellow, blue, and black. Out on the terrace Klah painted a "House Blessing" design which he left unfinished so that it could remain on the terrace a few days. It depicted the blue sun, corn, beans, squash, and herbs, with a bird above each plant and two bluebirds at the east. Klah was much amused when we stepped out on the terrace the next morning to see the design crisscrossed with tiny tracks of beetles, a mouse, a bird, and a trail that may have been made by a measuring worm or a caterpillar. He remarked that the "Little People" had blessed it. Many of Mary's friends were invited to see this example of Navaho religious art and to have its symbols explained to them.

One evening she held a reception with Klah as the guest of honor. The names of the guests looked like a page of Who's Who from Boston. Klah sang a few songs in Navaho to the rhythm of Clyde's drum. I gave a short talk on Navaho symbolism, showing several sand-painting sketches I had brought with me. In introducing us, Mary had spoken briefly on the subject of Navaho religion, stressing the fact that it still existed in its ancient form, since there had been little contact with white missionaries. As I gazed at the polite faces and the fixed smiles of the guests, I realized that this was just another lecture to most of them and carried no special meaning. It would be rated as "Mary's latest fad."

Our stay was made memorable by many jaunts to interesting homes and scenic places. A motorboat took us out to Rockefeller Island, where no autos were allowed, and we rode in a horse-drawn carryall along roads where a deer leaped across our path and we made a detour to avoid a fat badger that waddled along ahead of us.

There were wild huckleberries, quinaquina, wintergreen, and ground pine, with a background of moss and granite boulders. The trees were pine, spruce, and hemlock, with birch, larch, and poplar in the swales. I could name every tree, bush, and wild plant on the island, since this vegetation was exactly the same as I had grown up with in Wisconsin. We visited the Rockefeller home and walked through the wonderful Chinese garden, where ancient statues greeted us with fixed smiles or glared at us through stony eyes. Ray Murphy, Mary's cousin, invited us to an authentic "tea ceremony" in her Japanese teahouse. This building, of ancient design, had been the property of a Japanese nobleman, but Ray had purchased it, and expert builders had taken it apart, numbering each piece of wood as they did so. Then it was shipped to Maine, and the same experts reassembled it in Mrs. Murphy's Japanese garden.

As we came to the door, we were given satin sandals and kimonos to wear inside, where there were satin pillows on which to sit. A Japanese tea master conducted the ritual of heating the water, mixing the powdered tea, and serving it in the tiny Japanese bowls. It was quite an impressive rite, for there was complete silence.

As we were on our way home, Klah inquired, "Did that tea medicine man say a prayer when he mixed the tea medicine?"

"I did not hear any," I replied.

Then he asked, "What sickness is that tea ceremony used for?"

I tried to explain that it was not a healing rite, but just a ritual to make drinking of tea important. This he could not understand. To him, the sipping of a herb infusion should be connected with rites of healing, and he spoke of it as "the tea medicine ceremony" whenever it was mentioned.

Another friend of Mary's took us on an all-day yachting trip among the many small islands along the coast, stopping at a "fish house" for a lobster luncheon. They did not know that Navahos never eat fish of any kind, for they have been told their ancestors were turned into fish at the time of the flood. When we ordered, this presented a problem, but both Klah and Clyde were happy with ham and eggs.

Arthur enjoyed the fishing and was taken to several fishing areas in Mary's motorboat. When he finally hauled in a cod that was nearly four feet long, it was the highlight of the trip for him. He fished off the pier in the early mornings, and the fish he caught were seldom the same. This was a surprise to him, for in New Mexico there was only one kind of fish in a single place. On the first two mornings he brought his catch of five fourteen-inch snappers to the cook, but she threw them out saying they were not large enough to bother with. After that he threw fish of that size back into the ocean.

Klah was interested in all of the plants and bushes that

grew among the rocks and peaks. He examined leaves and blossoms, saying that one plant could be used for food and another for medicine, or perhaps another might be poison. But the ocean was the great attraction. We wandered along the shore picking up shells, odd stones, strings of seaweed, and bits of driftwood. One day he asked for a glass fruit jar, and, wading knee-deep into the water, he stooped and filled it with the sand, pebbles, and crushed shell that was under the water.

I asked why he wanted this and he answered, "It is a symbol of the land that holds the ocean and it is very powerful."

I asked if he was taking a little ocean water and he said, "Yes, that too is very powerful, but the earth that holds it is more important to us."

He was presented with many odd gifts by people who came to see us, and he collected many more items from both land and ocean, all of which we packed carefully and sent home by express.

One question Klah asked as we motored eastward was, "Where are all the Indians?" and he was greatly downcast when we were obliged to answer, "There are none here." In a span of four generations the hundreds of tribes that had ranged across the plains of Kansas and Nebraska, the hundreds more who had left their homes around the Great Lakes, and those who had raised their corn in the rich valleys of the central states had been decimated, scattered, and lost. Nothing but an occasional name remained to attest the fact that this land had once belonged to the American Indians. There still were a few Indians in Maine, and somewhere Mary found a very large Seneca and his very small

wife, both of whom she brought to visit Klah. But the interview was not exactly a success, as Klah wished to know
about their ancestors and the religion these ancients had
handed down to them. The visitors had lived too long among
the "palefaces" to have much to tell about tribal history or
the religion of their ancestors.

Klah enjoyed the two weeks in Maine very much. He
was always willing to go new places and meet new people
if Arthur could take him and if Clyde could be there to
answer his questions. Tina and "Staples," who was Mary's
chauffeur, were well-known friends, and I was there to tell
Klah where to go and which songs to sing, while Mary was
his friendly benefactor. Whether he ever realized how wide
an arc the pendulum of human economy swung on its journey from the Reservation in New Mexico, where Navaho
families often lived for days on a little parched corn and
were buffeted by every passing storm, to the other end of
the arc, where these Maine residents could choose any type
of native or imported food for their meals and whose wealth
formed a cushion to abate all annoyances, I do not know.

The two weeks passed rapidly, and on Monday morning we packed our luggage and ourselves into the car and
drove to Bangor. Here again the car was loaded into the
hold of the ship and we bought tickets to Boston. Here again
I was disappointed in the trip, for the boat, after leaving
the mouth of the river, put out to sea and we did not see
land again until we steamed in toward the Boston docks.
A fussy little tug eased us into a berth, and again we waited
for our car to be cleared and driven out to us. We found
a café on the docks while we were waiting, and the Indians
were greatly pleased when we ordered lamb stew, which

they had thought eastern cooks did not know how to make.

We were glad to leave Boston behind and drive toward the sunset. There would be a short stop in New York, and friends had secured a motor cabin near their home for Klah and Clyde. I wished to have a day in the city since I had bought nothing, so far, to take home to the girls or to the relatives who were caring for them. I found the big city a difficult place to shop, even with a city cousin for a guide, and it was three days before I finally had a supply of clothing and gifts for the girls and, scarfs and handbags for the aunts, and had ordered a fall outfit for myself to be sent later. My cousins had taken Klah and Clyde to Central Park and to the American Museum of Natural History, which they talked about a great deal as we drove along. It was a long slow day through Pennsylvania, and we were glad to stop early at a neat auto court at Youngstown.

The rain started when we were halfway across Ohio, and we drove slowly on slick roads. When we stopped for lunch in a small town, two or three people asked Klah to tell their fortunes. They would hardly believe me when I told them he was not a fortuneteller. In Indiana we started looking for a court or a small hotel that would take us in. Place after place said they had no vacancies or else there was a color bar. At ten o'clock, Arthur said he might as well drive all night, which he did, pulling off the road at one o'clock near a trucker's all-night café to rest an hour, eat excellent pie, and drink hot coffee. By daylight we had reached Gary and then drove into South Chicago, where we found tourist accommodations, scrubbed our hands and faces, ate breakfast, and then slept until noon.

After lunch I remained at the court while Arthur took

the two Indians to the La Salle Street depot, bought their tickets and sleeping accommodations on the Santa Fe to Gallup, New Mexico, staying with them in the station until they were safely on the train. We decided to stay where we were for at least a day, as the car needed some minor repairs and there was a garage handy. For once I was not interested in shopping, since the rain came at frequent intervals and the street looked gray and dismal. I spent the day repacking our luggage and the boxes I had acquired in New York. The next morning we headed for the summer resort in Wisconsin where the girls were staying. We had sent cards ahead, so they were expecting us and it was a happy reunion. They had reserved a two-bedroom cottage for our use, and it was wonderful to be a whole family again.

I asked Lynette if she had enjoyed her summer on the lake, and her answer was equivocal. Yes, she had learned to swim and could even dive off a low diving board. She had become acquainted with some youngsters of her own age and they had played tennis. But she did not like the deer flies and the mosquitoes. Then too, there were too many trees; a person couldn't look out and see anything.

Then I asked Priscilla the same question, and she was quite positive in her answer.

"This place is all right for a few days," she stated, "but I want to go home. I like paddling around the edge of the lake in the boat to catch poliwogs and small frogs and little shiny fish for my fish tank."

Here Lynette chimed in, "Yes, she just about lived in that boat, didn't even want to come in for meals."

I thought to myself that it was just as well I had not known that a little girl of eight years was alone in a canoe, day after day, paddling over deep water and along the shallow edges of the lake to dip up the poliwogs. It was a small lake, but grown men had been drowned there.

Priscilla continued, "And there was a bad thunderstorm and the lightning struck a tree across the lake and we all cried, and then I got real sick eating chokecherries, and I am all over covered with bites of mosquitoes and deer flies."

It was quite a tale of woe, but I suspected she was enjoying her recital.

It took us four days to say good-bye to all the Wisconsin relatives, and then we were on the road again. Even the car seemed eager to get home and the tires sang on the pavement. It had been a marvelous vacation, but when vacation time is over, it is wonderful to be on the way home.

16. Chicago and a Miracle

IT WAS MIDSUMMER OF 1931 when Klah's understudy, Beaal Begay, died quite unexpectedly, leaving Klah with no successor to his ceremony or to his vast collection of ceremonial articles. His own grand-nephews were away at school, and Klah felt that he was too old to take a young lad as neophyte and start teaching all over again. Beaal Begay had grown letter-perfect in chant, symbol, and rite of the entire Yeibichai Ceremony and was able to take the greater part of the nine-day ritual from Klah's shoulders, so his death was a sad loss. When Mary Wheelwright came from the East in the autumn, she asked Klah what he thought would happen to his ceremony and all of his paraphernalia, and he said he did not know. Then she asked if he would be willing to have it stored in a place where everyone could see it and study its use if they wished. Klah was much pleased with this idea, for he had already recorded many of his songs for her and I had made copies of more than fifty of his sand paintings. All of this would be in one place, safely housed for study by future generations.

Plans were made for the Museum of Navajo Ceremonial Arts. At first Mary thought it might be located on the campus of the University of New Mexico, in Albuquerque. She had the plans drawn for the building, which was to be built of logs in an octagonal form with a domed roof. The University authorities, however, refused to allow a structure of this type erected on the campus since all the other buildings were of Pueblo design and it would not be in harmony with them. Mary refused to alter the plans, so when Elizabeth White offered her some virgin land near the Museum of Anthropology in Santa Fe, she accepted this as the site of the Navaho Museum. From this time on, Klah brought us articles he had hidden away for many years. There was his grandfather's long war bow with the puma-hide quiver which contained two or three iron-tipped arrows; there were ancient rattles and prayer plumes; and there were baskets, arm bands, and amulets. All of these we were to keep in storage until the museum was ready for them. But Klah did not part with any of the things he might be called upon to use when he held any one of his four ceremonies.

In 1933, Anna Ickes came to our post for a three-day vacation from newspapers, telephones, and people. At that time she held the position of United States congresswoman from the state of Illinois and was very much concerned with the problem of Indian welfare. She realized that the aridity of the Navaho country was the chief hindrance to the self-support and prosperity of the Navaho people. She decided to visit the interior of the Reservation to see if anything could be done about storing or developing a greater and more dependable water supply.

Klah came the evening of the first day and told her how the country was losing the water of former years through less snowfall on the mountains, fewer summer rains, the silting of lakes and ponds, and the erosion of deep arroyos. He told her that underground water pressure was not as great as it once was, and that many places where there had been bubbling springs now had only a few green bushes. Mrs. Ickes was very much interested and asked Arthur if he would take her on a circle trip across the valleys and mesas east of the post, with Klah to point out the places he had mentioned. The next morning Klah came early and had hot cakes and coffee while I packed a lunch for them to take.

Since the only roads were the wagon roads of the Navahos and these often ended abruptly at a hogan or at the edge of a deep arroyo, it was slow traveling, but they saw a wide sweep of Indian country and came home in mid-afternoon, tired but still interested. Mrs. Ickes had been impressed by the many arroyos that cut deep gashes between the mesas and across the flatlands. "There must be a great deal of water at times to cut such deep channels in the soil," she said. "Where does it all go?" Arthur told her it came down from the mountains through the canyons and arroyos and emptied into the Río Chaco, which, in turn, emptied into the San Juan River. There were two seasons in which the arroyos often overflowed their banks—in the spring when the snows on the mountain melted, and again in midsummer during the summer rains.

"But is there no way the Indians can turn this water into their fields?" she wanted to know.

"Nearer the mountains they have lateral ditches and small cornfields, but down here the arroyos are too deep. They cannot bring the water up to field level," she was told.

"I would like to see the fields along the foot of the mountains," Mrs. Ickes said.

So the next morning the three set off again, this time toward the mountains at the west, and again they were gone the greater part of the day. Mrs. Ickes came home tired but excited. She had talked with a couple of traders and some Navaho farmers and all seemed to agree that much of the water could be utilized if a series of dams, beginning quite near the mountains and continuing at intervals down the arroyos, could be built. There would be no problem of silt, for it would be all the better if some of the deeper arroyos did fill, as the dams would be for diversion and not for storage. Klah did not join in the discussion and seemed doubtful the project would do much good.

Mrs. Ickes carried her movie camera wherever she went and had taken a short section of film of a little Navaho girl gathering green corn. She took another section of a man with a large watermelon, but when the camera started to whir, he froze in one position and did not move until it stopped. She told him to move about and tried again, but he did not understand, so his pictures were "stills" instead of movies.

Shortly after Mrs. Ickes returned to Washington, a crew of surveyors, sent by the Office of Indian Affairs, came to map the arroyos and mark the sites for the proposed dams. This crew seemed to be composed of young student survey-ors from Eastern colleges who were out on their first field trip. Or perhaps they were just the youthful relatives of some Washington politicians. At any rate, they were far and away too much educated to think of asking or taking the advice of the people living so far out in the "sticks." They hired Navahos with teams and scrapers, and in the next year they built dikes and dams and fills as their maps indicated, all of which looked wonderful on paper. But they built two of their longest dams across ditches that had carried no water for at least fifteen years. Another was built below the highway, and when the rains came the highway was flooded two to three feet deep for at least a quarter of a mile until the highway maintenance crew blasted a gap

Franc Johnson Newcomb and a photographer
examining Klah's last sand painting tapestry

MARY CABOT WHEELWRIGHT

in the dam. But the one that amused the Navahos most was built with the arc toward the mountains, as though they expected the water to come from the lower land and run uphill to fill the dam.

Some of the other valleys were luckier than we were, for their arroyos were successfully terraced and new cornfields were irrigated on either side. Thus, like many a government project, it could have been better, but then it might have been worse. However, the government had provided no funds for upkeep, and gradually the dams washed out or the water cut new channels beside the old arroyos and everything was the same as it had been before the terracing project was started. In 1935, Mrs. Ickes wrote that she would be out to visit us after the Gallup Ceremonial and the Hopi Snake Dance, as she wished to see the results of the water-diversion project. She did not live to make the trip, for she was fatally injured in an auto accident on the highway between Taos and Santa Fe on August 21, 1935. The Navahos lost one of their best friends with the passing of Anna Ickes.

It was May of 1934 when Arthur received a letter from state officials at Santa Fe saying that New Mexico was planning an Indian exhibit for the chief attraction in their state building at the Century of Progress Exposition in Chicago. They would like to engage a medicine man to go with a silversmith and a rug weaver, and they thought perhaps Klah would like to go and stay for three months. Arthur talked to Klah and explained that he would be expected to do some part of a sand painting every day and perhaps have his rattle handy to do a chant now and then. Klah thought awhile and then said, "Yes, I would like to go. When I was a young man I was at the first Chicago world's fair, and now I am old so that may be the last one I can attend. I will be ready whenever you say."

Arthur went to Gallup and bought him a suitcase and a small trunk. Klah bought velveteen for his sister to make three shirts of different colors, and Arthur fitted him to three pair of white trousers, which he did not seem to like. He bought several pieces of checked and striped calico and made trousers in the native fashion. He did not take all of his coral and turquoise beads, but he did wear a large silver concho belt, three strings of white shell beads, and two heavy turquoise bracelets. Tom Shorty was paid to make him a new pair of red deer-hide shoes with a large silver button on each, and I gave him three silk headkerchiefs in bright colors.

On the twenty-first of July we took Klah to Gallup, where he was to join the rest of the party and board the Santa Fe train for Chicago. Waiting at the Ceremonial headquarters in Gallup were Ah-Kena-Bah, the 250-pound Navaho weaver, and Fred Peshlaikai, one of the foremost Navaho silversmiths, who was an instructor of arts and crafts in the Navaho vocational school at Fort Wingate. The group created quite a stir at the Gallup station, as a large group of relatives, friends, and sight-seers had gathered to see them off. There were several cameras clicking or whirring, and several reporters jotting down last-minute remarks. One newspaper published the following item:

> Haughty Hosteen Klah, a 67 year old medicine-man from Newcomb, New Mexico, is making his third trip to Chicago—his second to a World's Fair at that place. Klah is the great grandson of old Chief Narbona, one of the great Navajo

war-chiefs who was never conquered by the white man. Klah said he wanted to go to this Fair to see what changes had been made in forty years and what new things the white people had thought of making.

Ah-Kena-Bah spoke English and had traveled with the 101 Ranch Wild West Show, but she was afraid of Chicago. She said, "I do not like all that whisky drinking and gun shooting. There must be none of that around me. I must have a quiet place to stay." When they found a room for her in a dormitory at Northwestern University, she was satisfied. The men also were housed in dormitories. At the New Mexico building Klah had a square about twelve by twelve feet fenced so that curious spectators could not crowd too close to him while he was working or step on the painting when it was finished. Klah and his sand painting were about the first things visitors saw when they entered the New Mexico building. In another small enclosure, Fred Peshlaikai had his forge, his chunks of bar silver, and his tools to demonstrate how the Navahos made their silver jewelry. At first Ah-Kena-Bah's loom was open to the guests, but so many picked up her balls of yarn and handled her weaving equipment that soon the management had a fence built around her exhibit also. In the main room of the New Mexico building there was a very fine exhibit of Indian arts and crafts from both Pueblos and Navahos, along with some very fine photographs of state scenes taken by Mr. Mullarky of Gallup and a book of sand-painting sketches by myself. It would be difficult to state how many people visited this exhibit, but someone gave Klah a guest book in which he asked people to sign their names. Among those who signed were the President of the United States, Franklin D. Roosevelt, and more than half of the governors of the individual states. This book was one of Klah's prize possessions in later years, and we often asked him to bring it to the post to show our guests.

Klah found the crowds tiring; he had never dreamed there could be so many people. He said, "Like leaves in front of a west wind." His little section did not get a breath of fresh air when it was surrounded by spectators, and he found his work uninteresting because it did not mean anything. Each day he made part of a painting which he destroyed at night, so it really had no purpose. In spite of the crowds, he was lonesome, for there were weeks at a time when he did not see a familiar face. The weather that summer was extremely hot and dry. Crops were burned to the ground in a dozen Western states. There were ninety deaths from heat in the city of Chicago alone, while for days the thermometer registered from 106 to 112 degrees. There was no such thing as air conditioning. The people in charge were kind and often took him around to visit other exhibits. He took great interest in the planetarium, since he was well versed in the star lore of Navaho mythology and this view of the planets brought many into view that he had been unable to see with the naked eye, but many of the other scientific wonders seemed useless to him. Finally he lost his appetite and was looking depressed, so the people in charge decided he had better go back to the Reservation, and they wrote Arthur that Klah was not feeling well. We had been a little worried about him because of the reports of the heat.

Since Lynette and Priscilla were away at school, it did not take us long to get the car serviced and packed and be on our way to Chicago. It was not a fast or a pleasant trip,

as we were caught in a couple of bad dust storms while
driving through the dust bowl and we lost one whole afternoon having the carburetor cleaned and the oil changed.
Across Kansas the farmers had abandoned their farms and
torn down their fences so that the livestock could roam
where they pleased in search of water. But there was no
water, and the bodies of dead animals dotted the landscape.
In two or three places, small bands of horses followed our
car for a mile or so, as though expecting food. Their only
food was dry and spiny tumbleweed, which, without water,
was worse than nothing.

On the fourth night from home we registered at the
Stevens Hotel and in the morning went directly to the fair-
grounds. The New Mexico building was easily located, since
all the state buildings were along one plaza. As we walked
along with the crowd, we saw Klah sitting on a bench under
the awning, his hands folded and his eyes on the ground.
I stepped in front of him and stopped, but he did not look
up. Then I held out my hand and said, "Hah-la Hah-ne Tse-
kis?" He evidently could not believe that he was hearing
Navaho words from a white woman. Slowly his gaze traveled from my feet up to my face, then he sprang to his
his feet and grasped my hand. He could not speak, and
tears were blinding both of us. Then he saw Arthur and
grabbed his hand and patted his shoulder. Never have I
seen anyone happier to see friends than Klah was at that
moment. We talked a while and Arthur told him we had
come to take him home, but planned to stay three or four
days to see the Exposition before starting on the return trip.
He went back to his sand painting with a cheerful face and
we watched for a few minutes; then, telling him we would

195

be back the next day, we went to find the manager of the New Mexico exhibit and tell him we had arrived to fix a date for Klah's departure. For four days we visited with Klah a few minutes each morning and spent the remainder of the day viewing the wonderful things that were on exhibit. But the heat was exhausting, and on the morning of the fifth day we drove to Klah's quarters, stowed his suitcase in the trunk of the car—his trunk had been sent by express—and headed for home. We took a northern route in order to miss the dust bowl and also to greet my aunts and uncles in Wisconsin. Klah was pleased to meet them again but asked where Arthur's people were. We told him that Arthur's mother lived in California. We stayed three days and then continued our journey.

On the way home Klah told us of the many things he had seen at the Exposition. He never tired of explaining the stars as he saw them through the great telescope at the planetarium. In his boyhood he had memorized the Tsonsoji or lesser Star Chant, and since that time had learned all there was to know of Navaho star lore, in which they grouped the stars in constellations somewhat the same as ours. To have these brought close enough to see the tiny stars which surrounded them was a great thrill. He told us that when First Woman placed the stars in the night sky, she used them to spell out all the laws that would be needed by the first people. These could not be written in the sand or on the water, since few people could see them there, but when they were written in the sky, everyone could look up and study them.

In Navaho star lore there are constellations named for all the animals mentioned in their mythology. There is the bear, the wolf, the porcupine, the badger, the chipmunk, the elk, the mountain sheep, the Gila monster, the lizard, the horned toad, the bumblebee, and many others. The five stars that form the "rabbit tracks" are called the "hunter's guide." When this constellation is in one position, the hunters lay aside their bows and arrows and remain at home. But when it tips to the east, the young of the deer and the antelope are no longer dependent on their mothers, and the hunting season begins. The coyote star in the south is the same as our "dog star," and the polar star is called "the campfire of the heavens."

When we arrived in Albuquerque, the girls were glad to see us. I remained with them, since we had rented a house there for the school year so that they could attend school there. When Arthur and Klah arrived in Gallup, they were again met by cameras and reporters, all eager to know what Klah thought of the Exposition. As reported in a 1934 Gallup newspaper, Klah said:

> The Americans hurry too much! All the time they hurry and worry as to how they are going to hurry and worry some more. They go through life so fast they have no time to see beauty or think deep thoughts. I am happier than white people because I don't have all those things to worry about. I live just the same as I did when I first went east in 1893, and when some possessions worry me, I give them away.

The summer of 1935 was not as hot or dry as the previous one had been. Now the sand-painting rugs woven by Klah and his two nieces were gaining renown. There were more orders than could possibly be filled, and the family was kept very busy. Klah's sister, Ahdesbah, spun most of the yarn, for Grandma Klah was now completely blind and so crippled with arthritis that she could barely move her hands. She died quietly in her sleep and was buried in her new clothing in the rocks where many of her family were already laid to rest. There is no period of mourning in a Navaho family for an aged person who has lived out his life span, for it is felt that the spirit is ready to travel to another world. Nor is there any dread of touching or handling the corpse of an old person as there is of that of a younger person. Prayers are chanted for four days as the spirit journeys along the Rainbow Trail—"Bikay-hozhun," "May the way be beautiful."

It was October, 1935, when my church guild in Albuquerque asked if I could arrange an Indian program for a church benefit. I told them I thought Klah would come and sing Navaho songs if they wished. The program was given on a Friday evening and my topic was "Symbols of the Navaho Sand Painting." Levi Kembel, an Oklahoma Indian with a very fine voice, sang "Pale Moon" and "Land of the Sky-blue Waters," and Klah sang short Navaho songs to the rhythm of his rattle. The affair was a great success. There was an overflow crowd and everyone wished to meet Klah and shake his hand. We were quite late getting home.

The next day being Saturday and a day off for the girls, we could accompany Arthur and Klah back to the Reservation. It was two hundred miles by way of Gallup, and much of the road was unpaved. The morning was cloudy with blustery fall winds, so we started early. It was a slow trip at best, but with rolling dust or rain showers it would take still longer. We had gone about forty miles when heavy, wind-blown clouds darkened the sky and hard gusts made driving difficult. Suddenly I looked across the mesa to my right and exclaimed, "What's that?" Everyone looked that way and Arthur said, "It's a cyclone!" He stopped the car and we watched the black hourglass column as it spun and swayed on a path that would take it across the road about a half-mile in front of us. We were already beginning to feel the side winds sucking in toward the center, when, to our horror, it turned directly toward us. We had all been standing in front of the car watching the progress of the funnel; now I told the girls to hurry and rushed to climb into the car. But not Klah. He started walking slowly toward the whirling mass, which was approaching with the sound of a thousand swarms of bees. Stooping now and then to pick up a pinch of earth or part of a desert plant, he put the accumulation into his mouth even while he was chanting. We could not very well turn around and go away, leaving him to face the tornado alone, and anyway, it was now much too late to make our escape, so we simply sat there—four of the most frightened humans anyone ever knew. Klah continued to walk slowly into the eddying wind, then suddenly held up both hands and spewed the mixture in his mouth directly at the approaching column and raised his voice to a loud chant. The column stood still for a moment and then divided in the center of the hourglass, the upper part rising to be obscured by the low hanging clouds and the lower half spinning away at right angles to its former course like a great upside-down top.

Klah turned around and came back to the car. Had we witnessed a miracle of faith? To this day, I believe we did. Later I asked Klah about the plants and the soil he had picked up, and he said, "The Spirit of the Earth is more powerful than the Wind Spirit." When we came to the place where the tornado had crossed the railroad track and the highway, many telephone poles had been torn out of the ground and splintered into kindling. Fence posts and the tangled wire blocked our way for some distance, while across the wide valley a great white gash appeared in the side of the high mesa. It was a very thankful Newcomb family who said their prayers that night, especially thanking the Almighty for a wonderful friend who would risk his life to save ours.

All through the summer of 1936, Klah's sister, Ahdesbah, had been in failing health. The Blessing Ceremonies and the Healing Chants that were held for her seemed to be of benefit for only a short time, then she became as weak as before. She gave up spinning and weaving and spent most of her time sitting or lying in the sun. Finally Klah took her to the Shiprock hospital for treatment by the agency doctor. Two of her daughters went with her and they stayed for about two weeks, when the doctor told them to take her home for there was nothing he could do to cure her. He said she had hemolysis, for which there was no cure.

Klah had made an engagement to hold a Yeibichai on the seventeenth of October, and Mary Wheelwright had come out to the trading post hoping that he would hold a Blessing Chant for Ahdesbah. But when the hospital car brought her to his cabin the next day, she was too ill to move, even her head. Klah realized there was no help for her, and he was much grieved and upset. I was in Albuquerque at the time, and Arthur wrote me: "Well, we could not get the ceremony put on, as Klah's sister was so terribly sick that I knew she would not live through the night, and she didn't. I went up to see her yesterday morning and I told

Mary there was no use planning a ceremony, and Klah felt the same. Then late last night he came for her beads and silver and bought new robes and other things, as she was dying. He felt very badly about it and so did I, as she was a fine old woman. He had a Yeibichai dated to start day after tomorrow but says it will have to be postponed."

Klah helped bury his sister and then stayed by her grave four days and nights to pray for the safe journey of her spirit. After Ahdesbah's passing, Klah was a very lonely person.

17. *The Rainbow Trail*

THE MUSEUM OF NAVAJO CEREMONIAL ARTS, being built in Santa Fe by Mary Wheelwright, was nearing completion. The structure itself had been finished and now the furniture was being carved, cabinets and cupboards were being built, and metal frames for displaying enlarged sand paintings were being installed. Already there was much valuable material in the storerooms. While Mary was there in the fall, we took Klah to see it and he was quite impressed and very much pleased that his sacred "medicine" would someday be housed there. He was especially pleased to find that the main part of the structure was built like a Navaho ceremonial hogan, with eight sides and a domed roof which had an opening on its eastern slant.

While he was there, Mary asked if he would permit a sculptor to carve a life-size bust of him in stone. Klah was a little hesitant at first, since that was something for which he had no precedent. But after thinking about it for a while, he agreed. Allen Clarke was living near Santa Fe at the time, and Mary engaged him to carve the bust. Three weeks later, Allen, his wife, and the largest great Dane I ever saw, came to our post and Allen asked Klah for the first sitting. He made his first model in clay and during their three-day stay, he produced a head and face that anyone could recognize as being that of Hosteen Klah. We had not counted on the effect this would have on our Navaho customers. As Mr. Clarke worked on the front porch, anyone could peer through the woven wire fencing and see him at work.

At first they did not realize what it was going to be, but the second day it began to take shape and then there was a commotion. They argued with Klah and they argued with Arthur saying that images of people should not be made. They said, "If that image is not pounded into dust, it will take Klah's spirit away from him and it will take his mind, then he will wander around without a mind and without a spirit and that clay image will cast an evil spell over all of us." They became so insistent that I had the bust put out of sight until the next morning when the Clarke's loaded it into their station wagon and departed. Arthur made arrangements to take Klah to Santa Fe for future sittings, about which the other Indians would know nothing. Klah looked very sober and thoughtful and I wondered if he, too, could be doubtful of the outcome. Arthur took him to Santa Fe several times that summer, but the bust was not completed for more than a year. It now occupies a prominent place in the museum that is dedicated to his memory, but the expression it records shows he was not pleased.

Late that autumn, when the girls and I were again living in Albuquerque and Mary had gone to Santa Barbara to enjoy the warm climate, she wrote to Arthur asking if Klah would like to come west to see the Pacific Ocean. Klah was delighted with the idea, as he said the immortals had come from a western land far out in the Great Water of the sunset. In the creation myth to which he referred it says: "When all the Indian tribes had been established on this present earth, the Sun said to Changing Woman, 'Your work here is finished; you must now go to the place of the sunset, where, far out over the great waters, I have built a house for you. I will send powerful guards with you—the Hail, the

Thunder, the Lightning, and the Water Ruler. The Wind, the Rain, the Clouds, and the Light have helped me make a beautiful house for you, and I wish you to live where I can meet you in the evening.' This house was built on a beautiful island called 'Land that Floats on the Water.' In it were four rooms on each of its four floors, for which there were ladders of black jet, white shell, turquoise, and abalone on the four sides. On top of the house there was a multicolored thunderbird, larger than any that has ever been seen, who was the chief of all thunderbirds. On his back he carried small thunderbirds of all the ceremonial colors. In the center of this palace was a large room with an altar decorated with all the colors of every flower that had bloomed and faded on earth, and with the spirits of all the birds. The main entrance was toward the east and was guarded by a white-shell rattle which gave the alarm whenever a visitor approached. To this place Changing Woman came to live forever and meet the Sun in the evenings."

Klah studied the map and decided the Channel Islands off the coast of Santa Barbara might be the ones mentioned in the myth. During the entire trip to the West Coast, Klah scanned the mesas and the peaks for landmarks his ancestors had described when they came from the West to find the promised land that was marked by the four sacred peaks. There was hardly a river valley or a high rocky range to which he did not give a Navaho name that was accurately descriptive. But through western Arizona and southern California he was surprised to find so little water. He had names for lakes, rivers, and small streams where there had been no water for hundreds of years. Between the Rockies and the Coast Ranges he described the ancient lakes and the Indians whose principle food was the root of the water lily. So this legendary journey must have taken place before the great drought of the eleventh and twelfth centuries changed the character of the Southwest. The devastating effect of a twenty-year drought cannot be estimated, and it must have caused many prehistoric tribes to separate and wander in different directions in search of food and water.

Klah found the Pacific Ocean even more interesting than the Atlantic. Again he gathered soil from under the water, yellow scum that stained the beach, and eight varieties of seaweed. He went with Mary and Arthur out to the Channel Islands and found some queerly shaped stones that had been used by ancient inhabitants. At the Santa Barbara Museum, the curator asked if Klah could give names to several oddly shaped stones that had been found on the islands, and he gave each a name and explained the games for which they had been used. There was not much writing or recording done on this occasion, although Mary wrote some of the *Creation Myth*. They visited so many places that there was little time left for writing, and after a ten-day stay, Arthur, Klah, and Clyde were on their way home. Of all the trips he had taken, I think Klah enjoyed the one to the Pacific Ocean the most. On the way home he was unusually quiet and thoughtful; finally he asked Arthur if there were other islands far out in the Ocean. When Arthur told him there were many, he brightened at once. The islands he had seen did not fit the description in the legend, as they were bare and gray. Changing Woman's island was described as a place where trees and beautiful flowers grew and there was no winter weather. He asked if some of the islands were covered with trees and green vegetation. Arthur told him that some were and others were just black volcanic rock. Then Klah was satisfied that somewhere in the vast Pacific there was a beautiful island where Changing Woman still lived in a shining cloud palace.

During the late summer of 1936 Klah presided at a Yei-bichai Ceremony in Arizona and while there became acquainted with two medicine men who knew the Water Chant. Mary had been trying for some time to find some trace of this ceremony which in past years had been the most important of all chants. We had been told that this was a lost ceremony, since the medicine man who sang it had died at the Bosque Redondo. So Mary was delighted to hear of medicine men who still knew at least parts of it. She asked Arthur to have the two chanters come to Newcomb and hold a Water Chant over anyone who needed that sort of ceremony. It was easy to find a patient, and we selected Ahson Hatile, whose hogan had been washed away in a flood. She was outfitted with new clothing, and all food and baskets for the ceremony were supplied and all expenses paid.

Getting the two medicine men was not so easy, for they were of the old regime and refused to have any white women witness their rites. Finally, Arthur took Klah and me over to Dinnehotso to meet them. I took presents and a couple of sand-painting sketches to show that I knew something of other ceremonies, and I spoke to them in Navaho. They still refused, so we left Klah to see what he could do while we built a fire, made hot coffee, and ate our lunch. When we talked to them again, they said to come back in two weeks and they would be ready to go. What arguments

Museum of Navajo Ceremonial Art, Santa Fe

INTERIOR OF THE MUSEUM
of Navajo Ceremonial Art showing drawings
from Klah's Yeibichai Ceremony

Klah had used in persuading them to change their minds, we will never know.

Our trading post had burned to the ground on May 9, 1936, taking our living quarters, the manager's house, the guest house, and all of the furnishings with it. When it came time for the water chanters to arrive, a new establishment was nearly completed. Of course, the store and the warerooms had been rebuilt first, so our accommodations for Mary were sketchy. She did not complain. As long as I was there to prepare the meals and there was some place to sleep, her whole interest was given to attending the rites, writing about the ritual, interviewing the medicine men, and so preserving as much of the Water Chant as possible. I memorized four beautiful sand paintings, the symbols on the prayer boards, and the design painted on the patient's body. It was well that we made this effort, for we never attended another Water Chant.

I did not see much of Klah for the next five months, except at Christmas time when we spent the two-weeks' vacation at the post, and then he was with us much of the time. Arthur said that he was so lonesome now that his sister was gone that he spent much of his time at the post. Sometimes he went to sleep in the big Morris chair in front of the fire and spent the night there. Arthur said, "When I set the table, I always put on a plate for Klah, as he is sure to be here sometime during the day."

It was a cold, stormy winter and there was much flu and pneumonia among the Navahos on the Reservation. Klah was called to sing the Apache Wind Chant or the Small Star Chant for many sick people all up and down the valley, and he was moving about in all kinds of weather.

He was growing older now and the effort of chanting all night over some sick person was almost too much for him, as his throat would fill up and his voice would almost fail. Although he knew it would be difficult, he seldom refused when someone came for him. Fulfilling the duties of a medicine man was his life's work, and he had no understudy to help him or to take his place if he refused to go.

It was on February 26, 1937, that I received a call from Arvil Witt, who then was the general manager of our trading post. He called to say that Klah was ill with pneumonia. "Where is Arthur?" was the first thing I asked.

"He has gone on a rug-buying trip and I am alone here with the store," Arvil replied.

I thought a minute and then said, "Lock the store and get Klah and take him to the Rehoboth Hospital, and take some of his relatives with him. I will phone the hospital to have a room ready for him."

Calling Dr. Pousma of the Rehoboth Mission, I found they could have a room ready for him and that there was a guest house where the relatives could stay. I was glad when they told me that the trained nurse who would care for him was a Navaho girl.

When the girls came home from school, I told them that I was going to Gallup for a few days and would have a woman stay with them. The next morning I packed my suitcase, drove to the hospital, and asked if there was a room in which I might stay. There were no guest rooms, but they moved the things out of one side of the linen room and put in a cot for me to use. They told me I could take my meals at the Mission dining room.

Klah was running a high fever and occasionally choking

with some throat obstruction. He knew me and asked for Arthur. I told him that Arthur would arrive in a little while. I was surprised at the number of relatives who were present to take care of him. There was Sam Velieto and Mrs. Sam, Irene and Jim, Daisy and her husband, Sam Foster and his wife, Chee Gould and his wife, and one or two more. There were always three or four sitting quietly in his room ready to answer his slightest wish, and I think this was the way he wanted it to be. The nurse was quiet and competent, speaking to him in Navaho so he knew what to expect when she took his temperature or gave him his medicine. He was somewhat better the next morning, but failing rapidly when Arthur arrived at noon. I asked Dr. Pousma if there was something more that could be done for him. He said, "No, we are doing all we can for him. His heart is greatly enlarged and is failing."

Klah asked for Arthur, who stood by his bed and held his hand. He then asked for his family to gather around him, and slowly, with many pauses for breath, he told them what he wanted done with his medicine bundles, sacred paraphernalia, and property. He asked Arthur to see that he had a "white" burial and asked his relatives to say the traditional prayers and chants for his departing spirit. His voice finally faded and he sank into a coma from which he did not wake, but it was well past midnight when the harsh breathing ceased and he was at rest.

It is customary among the Navahos to bury the deceased before sundown, as no member of the family, not even the babies, can partake of a morsel of food until after the burial. Arthur explained to the relatives that the burial could not take place until the next morning, but not to go without food for themselves or the children, especially the babies. Perhaps they did feed the small children, but none of the older members of the family ate an evening or morning meal. Arthur made all arrangements at the mortuary and bought a plot in the cemetery. He telephoned the mission at Tohatchi and asked the missionary to hold the graveside services. At ten o'clock the next morning, Klah's body was committed to the keeping of Mother Earth, to whom he had sung so many prayers while he was alive. Four of his male relatives camped among the trees above the cemetery and kept vigil for four days and nights, chanting the prayers that would accompany his spirit along the Rainbow Trail.

There were several reporters present, and the following item appeared in the Gallup paper:

March 3rd—(AP)—Hosteen Klah, powerful Navajo medicine-man master of a thousand pagan chants, was buried yesterday with Christian ceremonies. Only in death did Klah, regarded as the most powerful medicine-man, forsake the ritual of his religion. "It was in deference to his white friends," explained Arthur Newcomb, trader and friend of the Navaho singer. "He wished his burial to be in accordance with both the customs of the Indians and the white man." Thus Klah (the Left Handed) was laid to rest in a white man's cemetery after a brief white man's ceremony. But Navajo jewelry of turquoise, silver, jet, shell, and coral was heaped in his casket, every relative and friend giving something. Four self-appointed mourners joined Klah's relatives in four days of fasting. The Indians as they left the cemetery were careful not to cross the trail of the funeral caravan lest the spirit of the dead return to plague them.

Famed as sand-painter, herb doctor, and chanter, Klah took to the grave many sacred Navaho prayers and rituals. Recognized several years ago as the last to know many of the older chants such as the "Hail Chant," the "Rain Chant," and the "Apache Wind Chant," he was persuaded by Arthur Newcomb to have them recorded. Klah's understudy, Beaal Begay, died several year ago and the Indian leaders say there is now none to succeed him.

And so Klah's passing was taken note of by newspapers around the world.

Another reporter had this to say:

Rehoboth Mission, March 3rd—(AP)—The spirit of the greatest of Navajo medicine-men winged a weary journey around the world today, and with it went many a precious secret of the tribe's religious life. Four times, says Navajo religion, the soul of Hosteen Klah will encircle the Earth— four times for the four directions of the compass—and then it will soar away to a world beyond to reside in peace and beauty. For Hosteen Klah, kindly, gentle, beloved, and versed in spiritual knowledge as no other Navajo of his time, is dead at the age of 70 and the sacred chants he alone knew died with him yesterday.

The Southwest Tourist News published the following article which summarizes the story of his life:

Hosteen Klah, venerable medicine-man of the Navajo tribe, died Tuesday at Rehoboth Mission near Gallup, taking with him the secrets of his profession. His understudy died a few years ago and Klah never had undertaken to train another youth to fill his place. Klah was 70 years old. In his time he had traveled to two World Fairs in Chicago, the first in 1892 when he was a young man and the second in 1934. He spent his time at the last Fair in the New Mexico State Building making sand-paintings. Some of these sand-paintings have been conserved by Mrs. Arthur Newcomb of Albuquerque, white woman student of Navajo religion and friend of Klah for many years.

Recordings of his chants have been collected by Miss

Mary Wheelwright of Boston and of Alcalde, New Mexico, another student of Southwestern Indian lore. Klah was a picturesque figure. When the Crown Prince of Sweden stopped at the Newcomb trading-post on his way across New Mexico, he took several pictures of Hosteen Klah. His trips to visit the four great water boundaries, the Atlantic Ocean, the Gulf of Mexico, the Pacific Ocean, and the Great Lakes, were made with his trader friend, Arthur J. Newcomb. Klah was the great grandson of the well known Chief Narbona, the greatest of Navajo war chieftains. Narbona was 83 years old when he was shot by the soldiers of the Simpson Expedition, which had been sent by the United States government to make a treaty of peace with the Navajos.

I sent a telegram to Mary, who was staying with friends in Florida at the time, and received the following reply: "A great man has passed. I send sympathy to his family and to you."

When Gladys Reichard of Barnard College was told of his death, she said, "He was the gentlest man I ever knew."

An Indian trader's wife who knew him well said, "There never was a kinder man."

And Arthur Newcomb mourned his passing, "He was the best friend I ever had."

As for myself, I was grieved at his passing and also grieved that so much unrecorded knowledge should be lost forever. But I would not have wished him to live to see the time he could not chant the prayers or hold the ceremonies which had become such an important part of his life.

So the chapter closes on the life of a great, good, and learned man. But I doubt if "finis" will ever be written to the influence he left with his family, his friends, and the many people he sought to heal or benefit with his great spiritual faith.

18. The Museum

THE STORY OF HOSTEEN KLAH'S LIFE cannot end without including the story of the beautiful museum that was erected to preserve his medicine lore and all the symbolic articles that pertained to his religion. The structure itself was fashioned as nearly like a Yeibichai ceremonial hogan as the architect could plan it and still have it large enough to display the sand paintings, rugs, tapestries, cases of ceremonial articles, clothing, jewelry, and everything pertaining to Navaho life and religion. The building consisted of two stories, the upper part being the "hogan," the eight sides of which are built of beautifully matched logs with a projecting portico to the east. The roof is dome shaped with a large window slanting to the east to admit the morning sunlight. This morning light shines down on a permanent sand painting which is made on a base that stands somewhat to the west of the center. Six of the wall spaces contain large copies of sand-painting sketches, which can be changed to accord with the season or with the topic that is under discussion. The lower floor is entered only from the east and contains the exhibit rooms, the study, several storage rooms, and an apartment for the curator.

Klah did not live to preside at the dedication ceremony, which would have been a great event in his life if he had been there. But everyone who attended this ceremony felt that he was not far away—nor was he. After Mary came back to Alcalde, she asked Arthur if he could get permission from Klah's relatives to have his casket disinterred and reburied on the knoll beside the museum. This took some time, for it was difficult to explain to the relatives why anyone would wish to disturb a burial. They wanted to know if the casket would be opened so that someone might steal the jewelry and medicine bundles it contained. Arthur assured them that not even the rough box on the outside would be opened. They then wanted to know if anyone would try to take pictures or if there would be a news item in the papers about it. Arthur told them it could be done quietly with no one except the men who were hired to do the digging and the funeral director knowing anything about about it. The funeral director would get permission to move the casket and would change his burial records. Finally they all agreed, but insisted they did not wish to know when it actually took place, as they did not care to know when his body was above ground.

So Mary sent a hearse from Santa Fe, and Klah's casket was taken to the knoll beside the museum and buried in an unmarked grave. Later that fall, she asked that we have several wild plants and herbs that Klah had been in the habit of gathering for his ceremonies carefully dug and transplanted around his resting place. These plants were the giss-dil-yessie (desert goldenrod), the tohe-kath (water grass), the tsey-yeh-zhe (grass daisy), and the dlah-has-tazzie (dwarf sage). From these and others he had brewed his tonics and his emetics.

At the time of his death Klah had a large sand-painting tapestry, two-thirds completed, on his loom. Mrs. Sam, Mrs. Jim, and Daisy completed this rug and brought it to Arthur to repay the funeral expenses, the robe and clothing that had been bought during his illness, and the pawned beads, silver belt, coral, and turquoise that had been buried with him. I still have this rug, the last work done by Klah, and, since my daughters wish to keep it, it will remain in our family for at least another generation.

Mary paid the relatives for the medicine bundles, prayer plumes, rattles and other articles that belonged to the Hail Chant, and I had been given nearly all that belonged to the Blessing Rites before Klah died. I also acquired the Wind Chant bundles, all of which I placed in the museum. During the past years, I had made copies of more than sixty of the sand paintings in my collection that were taken from Klah's ceremonies and had given them to the museum. These were from the six ceremonies Klah had knowledge of, but the majority were from the Yeibichai Chant.

Mrs. Sam decided to keep all the Yeibichai medicine in hopes that her son, Harry, might study the rites and become a medicine man. But when he went away to school, she gave up that idea. About that time, distant medicine men came to her asking to borrow the prayer plumes, or the rain rattles, or the Yei masks, and she could not refuse to loan them. We were quite upset when we heard about this and knew that, sooner or later, Klah's Yeibichai equipment would be scattered and lost. We talked to Mrs. Sam and found that two very old rattles and a few other small articles were missing, so she and Sam brought it all over to our storeroom until Mary could come the next fall and make arrangements to buy it. There were three trunks filled to the brim and also some long stiff leather rolls (buffalo) that held bamboo, pampas grass stalks, and other long articles. The most valuable part of the collection were the masks and the buckskins. There were the two white masks with twelve eagle feathers attached to each that were worn by Hastiji-altai (Talking God) and Hastji-hogan (House God). There were twelve buckskin masks for the Yei dancers, a black one marked with stars for the Fire God, a blue one for the Water Sprinkler, two with horns for the Humpbacked Ones, two for the Fringe Mouths, and several extras. There were rolls of sacred buckskins which had been obtained by smothering the animals with pollen to keep their blood from being shed. There were ceremonial baskets, prayer sticks, and mixtures of herbs, paints, and pollens. There were abalone shells, prehistoric arrowheads, and small pottery bowls. In fact, it was a lifetime collection of articles that might be symbolic of some magic power.

There was a bit of rock that symbolized the power held by the crest of a high mountain, and there was sand from under the waters of two oceans. There was magic from the tip of a tall tree and from the roots of a lowly plant the Navahos call "Earth's Hair." There was pollen from trees and flowers, feathers from many varieties of birds, fur from land and water animals, and shells from turtles and clams. There was the huge, coiled horn of a mountain ram, the stiff-haired mane of an elk, and a buffalo pelt, each article symbolizing some phase of the spirit's power.

Who could compute its value? To a medicine man who knew its use, it would be worth a fortune, but to the un-initiate it would be valueless, and some of it could be used only by the person who had gathered it.

Mary looked at the collection without touching any object, then made the nieces an offer which was quietly accepted. We knew that their answer would be a calm "Yes" or "No," as there must be no contention over Klah's sacred medicine. I think Mary realized this and offered more than had been expected so everyone would be satisfied. Arthur wrapped the smaller bundles in a canvas bag and hired a truck to take it all to the museum, where part of it has been put on display and the rest is safely stored.

Later the same year, Mary decided to have the museum dedicated by the Navaho method called the "House Blessing Ceremony," which the Indians use for any new dwelling or structure before living in it. Mary had planned this ceremony before Klah's death and now went ahead with her plans by asking Klah's nephew, Big Man's Son, to act in his place. A very good article describing this dedication appeared in the *Santa Fe New Mexican* at that time:

> The House of Navajo Religion, the octagonal Indian hoghan which Mary Cabot Wheelwright has built on her property adjoining that of the Laboratory of Anthropology, to house a collection of some 400 sand-paintings, was privately dedicated yesterday by a group of twenty-one Navajo Indians. The building will stand as a memorial to the most noted medicine-man of the Navajo reservation, Hosteen Klah, who died in February of this year. Klah, who had acted as Miss Wheelwright's informant for some fifteen years on the reservation, was represented by about fifteen nieces and nephews, grand-nieces and grand-nephews at the ceremony held Sunday. He had never married so these are his nearest remaining relatives. The ceremony that blessed the Museum was the "House Sing," the same that is used by the Navajos in blessing their own homes. Four Navajo songs were sung to ask blessings from the four directions, led by Bigman Begay, a grand-nephew, and interpreted by Clyde Beaal, a distant relative, brother of Beaal Begay who had been Klah's understudy. During the last song of the Hoghan Beyien, Clyde took pollen from a little pouch, motioning up the walls

to the shrine in the east, he tossed a little pollen, then to the south, the west, and to the north, to give the actual pollen blessing to the walls of the house. Then a thin-lined cross on the floor and a circle around, and lines across the ceiling as pollen is the Navajo blessing symbol. The final song mentioned the earth and the sky, the sun and the moon, the stars, clouds, and winds asking their spirits to stand guard over this house and bring it peace.

At the request of Mrs. Arthur Newcomb, the person who has collected all the sand-paintings for this museum, the Indians sang the "Traveler's Song" for Miss Wheelwright who will be leaving soon on a trip to the Orient and not return until next March. Also for Mr. and Mrs. Newcomb who will be traveling east. This song is a prayer for a happy journey and a pleasant path for the travelers, with peace above and around them as they travel along.

The ceremonies Sunday were not only by, but for, the Indians as Miss Wheelwright wishes them to feel that this is their building, and feel free to visit it and perhaps learn of ancient rites now lost to them.,

"Klah had planned to hold this ceremony," she said, "before any of his things had been put in it. Next spring after the sand-paintings are all in place the public will be invited for a formal opening."

Sunday the 21 Indians sat on the floor at the south side of the big room, while Miss Wheelwright and a few intimate friends, also the workmen who constructed it, were seated on the north in the customary manner of the reservation. Among the few white persons attending were William P. Henderson, the architect, his wife, Alice Corben Henderson, Mr. Newstrom of the contracting firm and Mr. and Mrs. Arthur J. Newcomb, white traders from the Navajo reservation with whom Miss Wheelwright has stayed throughout years of travel there.

Miss Wheelwright sent a bus to the reservation to bring the Indians to Santa Fe and they lived in the "hoghan" during their stay here, cots being put up in the exhibit and the storage rooms for their sleeping quarters. They were not dressed in ceremonial costumes but in their every-day colorful clothing, and during the service the men removed their hats, replacing them with brightly colored kerchieves. Many of those attending were medicine-men of the Navajo tribe. Ahson Hathili, an elderly woman who is the only practicing "medicine-woman" on the reservation was among those present, also Peshlikai, the silver-smith.

The building in Santa Fe is based on the old style ceremonial "hoghan." It is much larger, however, and built of logs and cement. The shrine on the eastern wall showing the sun above and the corn below, was designed by Klah before his death. The tri-colored arc-decoration encircling six sides of the eight-sided walls near the ceiling, is representative of the rainbow and was carved by Gregorio, a Spanish-American of New Mexico. Solid Vigas form the ceiling, 160 huge logs stretching up the eight sides and across the vaulted top. The door is at the east as is typical of all Navajo hoghans, and from it, steps circle around on either side to the main exhibit hall. Light is furnished by a skylight in the ceiling, slanted to the east to catch light from the morning sun, and allow a mid-day beam to rest on the eastern altar.

Miss Wheelwright plans construction of two actual hoghans near this glorified model, one in the traditional shape which was the inspiration for this, and one more modern without the opening in the roof. [These were never erected.]

The collection of sand-paintings and enlargements is not yet complete, however, some 300-odd paintings are ready to put in place. There will be one permanent painting in sand in a low case, to show the actual technique. This painting was taken from the Big House Ceremony, commonly, but incorrectly known, as the "Shooting Chant." Most of the sand-paintings in the building will be of card-board size 22 by 28 inches but some will be enlarged to eight by eight feet to approximate the size of a real sand-painting. Steel frames in the basement will hold the enlargements, which can be brought up through an opening in the floor by a hand-operated lift, when they are to be exhibited. The paintings will be hung in rotation, the exhibit being changed possibly every month.

In the following years, many ceremonial artifacts and Navaho sand paintings have been added to this primary collection. These were obtained from Navaho medicine men from every part of the Reservation, partly by myself and partly by other collectors. Mary also brought a few religious articles and symbols from other parts of the world for comparative purposes.

Mary Wheelwright died on August 2, 1958, at her summer home on Sutton Island off the Maine coast. She left a substantial endowment for the museum, and friends have added to this amount, so the care and upkeep, the publishing, and the collecting can still be continued. Under the supervision of the present curator, Kenneth Foster, many of Mary's plans have been carried to completion and many of her writings published.

As the years pass, the Navaho people will come more and more to accept the education, the customs, and the religion of their conquerors, and then the old ways and the old beliefs will be forgotten. But much of the past will be preserved in the uniquely beautiful Museum of Navajo Ceremonial Arts that stands as a memorial to two great people, Mary Cabot Wheelwright and Hosteen Klah.

Bibliography

NEWSPAPERS

The Farmington Hustler
The Gallup Independent
The Santa Fe New Mexican
The Southwest Tourist News

ADDITIONAL REFERENCES

Coolidge, Dane and Mary. *The Navajo Indians.* Boston and New York, Houghton Mifflin Company, 1930.

Gregg, Josiah. *Commerce of the Prairies,* ed. by Max L. Moorhead. Norman, University of Oklahoma Press, 1954.

Simpson, Lieut. James H. "Report of an Expedition into the Navajo Country," in *Reports of the Secretary of War,* 31 Cong., 1 sess., *Senate Exec. Doc. 64.* Washington, printed at the Union Office, 1850.

Twitchell, Ralph E. *The History of the Military Occupation of the Territory of New Mexico.* Denver, Smith-Brooks Company, 1909.

Van Valkenburg, Richard. *A Short History of the Navajo People.* Window Rock, Arizona, U.S. Indian Service (mimeographed), 1938.

Index

University of Oklahoma Press

Norman